MODERN HUMANITIES RESEARCH ASSOCIATION
CRITICAL TEXTS
VOLUME 80

THE PEN AND THE NEEDLE:
ROUSSEAU & THE ENLIGHTENMENT DEBATE
OVER WOMEN'S EDUCATION

MODERN HUMANITIES RESEARCH ASSOCIATION
CRITICAL TEXTS

The MHRA Critical Texts series aims to provide affordable critical editions of lesser-known literary texts that are out of copyright or are not currently in print (or are difficult to obtain). The texts are taken from the following languages: English, French, German, Italian, Portuguese, Russian, and Spanish. Titles are selected by members of the distinguished Editorial Board and edited by leading academics. The aim is to produce scholarly editions rather than teaching texts, but the potential for crossover to undergraduate reading lists is recognized.

Editorial Board
Chair: Professor Katherine Astbury (University of Warwick)
English: Dr Stefano Evangelista (University of Oxford)
French: Professor Katherine Astbury (University of Warwick))
Germanic: Professor Ritchie Robertson (University of Oxford)
Hispanic: Professor Ben Bollig (University of Oxford)
Italian: Professor Jane Everson (Royal Holloway, University of London)
Portuguese: Professor Stephen Parkinson (University of Oxford)
Slavonic: Professor David Gillespie (University of Bath)

texts.mhra.org.uk

The Pen and the Needle

Rousseau & the Enlightenment Debate over Women's Education

Edited by Joanna M. Barker

Modern Humanities Research Association
Critical Texts 80
2021

Published by

*The Modern Humanities Research Association
Salisbury House
Station Road
Cambridge CB1 2LA
United Kingdom*

© *Modern Humanities Research Association 2021*

Joanna M. Barker has asserted her right under the Copyright, Designs and Patents Act 1988 to be identified as the author of this work. Parts of this work may be reproduced as permitted under legal provisions for fair dealing (or fair use) for the purposes of research, private study, criticism, or review, or when a relevant collective licensing agreement is in place. All other reproduction requires the written permission of the copyright holder who may be contacted at rights@mhra.org.uk.

First published 2021

ISBN 978-1-83954-122-3

CONTENTS

	Introduction	1
1	Jean-Jacques Rousseau *Émile, or Education*	3
2	James Fordyce *Sermons for Young Women*	15
3	Hester Chapone *Letters on the Improvement of the Mind*	24
4	Stéphanie de Genlis *Adelaide and Theodore, or On Education*	36
5	John Bennett *Strictures on Female Education*	47
6	Catharine Macaulay Graham *Letters on Education*	60
7	Maurice de Talleyrand *Report on Public Education*	70
8	Mary Wollstonecraft *A Vindication of the Rights of Woman*	77
9	Maria Edgeworth *Letters for Literary Ladies*	87
10	Thomas Gisborne *An Enquiry into the Duties of the Female Sex*	96
11	Priscilla Wakefield *Reflections on the Present Condition of the Female Sex*	104
12	Mary Hays *An Appeal to the Men of Great Britain in Behalf of Women*	111
13	Hannah More *Strictures on the Modern System of Female Education*	120
	Conclusion	131
	Bibliography	132

INTRODUCTION

The intellectual and philosophical movement known as the Enlightenment reached its height in the middle of the eighteenth century. It incorporated many strands of thought, but its main principle was the discovery of truth through the use of reason. Its practitioners questioned beliefs that relied for their authority on sacred documents or the antiquity of institutions, and if they considered them inadequate to deal with contemporary reality, called for them to be reformed or replaced.

One of the questions that had fascinated people for centuries was the nature of women. By the beginning of the period covered by this compilation, it was generally accepted that women were vain, frivolous and superficial, driven by their emotions and dangerously prone to scandalous behaviour. The only question was whether these undesirable traits were inherent, or the result of inadequate education. Those who espoused the former view could see the solution only in terms of putting women under strict supervision, while the latter group tried to devise a way of training women to impose the required discipline on themselves.

This collection contains thirteen textual extracts from books written on the subject of women's education. They are arranged in chronological order of first publication, and show how the controversy developed over the forty-year period from 1760 to 1800, a time of dramatic political and social change. The most significant break from the old order was the French Revolution; its principles of liberty were greeted with enthusiasm by many in Britain, but when the Revolution turned to regicide, terror and war, as well as the stamping out of organised religion, the nation's authorities felt it necessary to crush all such demands, for fear that the smallest innovation might overthrow the whole edifice.

The debate over the role of women in society was caught up in this torrent of excitement. Some women adopted the language of rights and freedoms to claim that they were also in need of liberation from the rule of men, but the backlash from the French Revolution discredited their radical ideas, which were in any case espoused only by a minority. Other women, themselves socially conservative, struggled to devise an educational programme fitted to women's domestic destiny that would permit those defined as 'exceptional' (including themselves) to appear in the public eye through their writing.

This collection includes the writings of five men and eight women, and sets them in the context of their time and place. Most of the authors were English or Irish but three were French, and this is significant, for the interchange of ideas between Britain and France was at the time very strong. And perhaps the most influential of all was the man with whom we start: Jean-Jacques Rousseau.

Note on the Texts

The texts are transcribed from editions published during the lifetime of their authors; these may be a later edition than the first, particularly where the author added new material. The translations of Rousseau and Talleyrand are my own.

— 1 —
Jean-Jacques Rousseau

Rousseau's views on education, and on the relationship between the sexes, were so influential that anyone in Europe who wrote on the subject in the second half of the eighteenth century was in some sense arguing with him. His book *Émile, or Education* was first published in 1762[1] and enjoyed a *succès de scandale*, being condemned to be burned in both Paris and Geneva for its anti-clerical statements. This naturally made people even more keen to read it, and it was immediately pirated by other booksellers, who issued it under false imprints to avoid the censors. It was regularly reprinted throughout the century, with twelve more editions before 1790.

Émile enjoyed equal success in Britain. The first English translation came out almost immediately,[2] and there were eight editions in London, Edinburgh and Dublin in the following thirty years. Rousseau's influence can be discerned even in the case of writers who did not mention his name or who disapproved of his views on religion or politics, and some female commentators openly attacked him.

Jean-Jacques Rousseau (1712–1778) was already a celebrated author by the time he published *Émile*. He first came to the attention of the public in 1750 by winning an essay prize on the subject of the arts and sciences, in which he expressed the contrarian view that the progress of culture and learning does not lead to the improvement but to the corruption of society.[3] Rousseau's belief that humanity had been at its best at a time when people lived in simple agrarian societies was further developed in his *Discourse on Inequality*, published in 1754.[4] In his view, inequality was caused by the development of private property and the corrupting effect of luxury, and also by a 'rage for distinction' which motivated a thirst for knowledge and caused people to compete for fame, glory

---

[1] Jean-Jacques Rousseau, *Émile, ou de l'Éducation* (The Hague: Jean Néaulme, 1762). This was a false imprint: it was actually published in Paris by Duchesne but without the necessary official permission.

[2] Jean-Jacques Rousseau, *Emilius and Sophia, or A New System of Education*, trans. by William Kenrick (London: Becket & De Hondt, 1762).

[3] Jean-Jacques Rousseau, *Discours sur les Sciences et les Arts* (Geneva: Barriot, 1750).

[4] Jean-Jacques Rousseau, *Discours sur l'origine et le fondement de l'inégalité parmi les hommes* (Amsterdam: Marc-Michel Rey, 1755).

and high office. It would have been better for humanity to have remained in a state of happy ignorance.

In the same year that saw the publication of *Émile*, Rousseau brought out what would become his most influential work of political philosophy, *The Social Contract*.[5] In it he recognised that humanity cannot return to a state of nature — our innocence, once lost, cannot be regained — but suggested that institutions could be created in the modern world that would enshrine the principles of liberty and equality. Rousseau rejected the theory expressed by John Locke and others, that existing governmental institutions represented the free agreement by individuals to put themselves under someone else's authority.[6] In Rousseau's view, to renounce liberty was to renounce humanity and render morality impossible, since moral behaviour must by definition be freely chosen. *The Social Contract* was to become one of the founding texts of the French Revolution.

Émile was Rousseau's attempt to illustrate how a man could live virtuously in a corrupt society. The masculine noun is deliberately chosen here, since the book makes it explicit that his views on liberty, equality and moral autonomy related only to men. The book takes the form of a fictionalised account written by the tutor who takes charge of Émile soon after he is born and has him brought up in the countryside, far from the evils of the city. Rousseau is explicit in insisting that his aim is to train a man and not a citizen: he is not interested in preparing his pupil for a profession or a position in society. Émile will be taught to be honest and generous and virtuous, but this is not all; the most important goal in life is for a man to learn to be independent and self-reliant. Émile will be a free spirit, secure in the knowledge of his own self-worth, and not dependent on the opinions of others.

Before *Émile*, the most influential European work on the bringing up of children was John Locke's *Some Thoughts Concerning Education*.[7] Locke had already promulgated the view that at birth the human mind did not contain any innate ideas: it was like a blank sheet of paper.[8] (This was controversial, since it denied that the mind contained a natural apprehension of God.) The development of ideas arose from the operation of reason on sensation: children observe things in the external world and work out the connections between them. Complex thought arises from the 'combination' of simple ideas.

Rousseau acknowledged the influence of Locke, and his plan of education

---

[5] Jean-Jacques Rousseau, *Du Contrat Social, ou Principes du Droit Politique* (Amsterdam: Marc Michel Rey, 1762).
[6] John Locke, *Two Treatises on Government* (London: Andrew Millar for Thomas Hollis, 1688).
[7] John Locke, *Some Thoughts Concerning Education* (London: A. & J. Churchill, 1693).
[8] John Locke, *An Essay Concerning Human Understanding* (London: Thomas Bassett, 1690), Book II.

was designed not to instruct his pupil but to guide him; not to fill his head with facts and concepts he cannot understand, but to teach him how to learn. Émile absorbs discipline by coming up against natural limitations rather than through reward and punishment. He is never made to learn anything by heart, since rote learning is pointless. In fact, his early education is merely 'negative', and consists of passing time in healthy outdoor pursuits while waiting for his faculties to develop. He is left to work things out for himself, rather than having other people's ideas imposed on him.

An entirely different set of principles applied to women, for 'women were especially created to please men'. This did not mean all men: apart from their physical destiny of bearing and caring for children, women's function was to live a life of retired domesticity, charming and entertaining their husbands and their family circle. Any attempt by women to compete with or dominate men, or to involve themselves in literature or politics, was to be severely quashed, since this would mean they were acting against nature and were therefore corrupt. It would also make them unhappy, as they struggled against their natural instincts to create a false 'masculine' personality.

Today we would characterise these views as misogynistic, but Rousseau would have been horrified by any suggestion that he was against women. On the contrary, he adored women who acted correctly — that is, according to their prescribed nature — and was confident that what he proposed was in their best interests. In the year before *Émile* appeared, he published *Julie, ou La Nouvelle Héloïse*,[9] which illustrated his views on the correct relationship between the two sexes in fictional form. Julie, the heroine, has a brief affair as a young girl but repents and becomes the wife of an older man, submits to his authority, and devotes herself to the upbringing of their children. The family moves far away from the corrupting city and establishes an enclosed community with their servants and her former lover, who is appointed her children's tutor. Their continuing strong feelings for each other are the basis for the story's dramatic tension, until Julie dies of a fever caused by rescuing her young son from drowning.

Julie was Rousseau's most popular work, and indeed was the biggest bestseller of the century: publishers could not print copies fast enough, so they rented the book out by the day or even by the hour. There were at least seventy editions published before 1800, and it made Rousseau into an international celebrity.

The views about the role of women expressed in the novel are just as restrictive as those in *Émile*, yet it was enormously popular with women readers. To understand this, it is necessary to recognise that among the French upper classes, and the bourgeoisie who aspired to imitate them, women had

---

[9] Jean-Jacques Rousseau, *Julie, ou La Nouvelle Héloïse* (Amsterdam: Marc Michel Rey, 1761).

been regarded as having little function beyond being child-bearing machines: Diderot mused that he couldn't really see the point of women continuing to exist once they had stopped being attractive to men.[10] Babies were handed to wet-nurses as soon as they were born, and left to the care of servants until it was time for the boys to be sent to college, while girls were put into convents where they frequently learned little beyond reading, writing and needlework; they would be taken out in their late teens and married to a man chosen by their parents for reasons of wealth, status or family convenience. For lack of an occupation, high-status women filled their lives with *divertissements*: theatre, balls, assemblies, gambling at cards and love affairs. Being forced to stay at home would be to die of boredom, and being sent away from Paris to the countryside was regarded as a sentence of exile.

Rousseau particularly loathed literary women and could be moved to fury by the Parisian salons, where women presided over men and sat in judgment over their literary works. Later in *Émile* he made this very clear:

> I would a thousand times prefer a simple girl with a basic education to a learned lady and wit who would set up a literary tribunal in my house and make herself its president. A woman with intellectual pretensions is the scourge of her husband, her children, her friends, her servants, of everyone. From the sublime heights of her great genius, she despises all her feminine duties [...] Outside her home she is always ridiculous and quite rightly criticised, as we cannot fail to be as soon as we step outside our proper sphere into one for which we are not fitted [...] What would make you think better of a woman when you enter her room, what would cause you to greet her with greater respect: to see her occupied with her womanly tasks and household duties, mending her children's clothes; or to find her writing poetry at her dressing-table, surrounded by piles of pamphlets and tinted notepaper? If the world were peopled only by wise men, literary women would remain spinsters all their lives.[11]

The power of Rousseau's novel was that it exalted motherhood as not only a valued role but a sacred trust: by taking responsibility for the early moral education of their children, women carry out a function that is important not only for their own families but for the whole of society. He offered women a new and flattering image of themselves, and a model that women of different social and economic backgrounds could adopt. Julie is the centre of her household and her husband and children love and respect her. We may observe, however, that her early death was not only a satisfying dramatic denouement but also a means for Rousseau to avoid tackling the tricky question of what would become of her once her children had left home.

---

[10] Letter to Sophie Volland, 15 August 1762, cited in Elisabeth Badinter, *Mme du Châtelet, Mme d'Épinay, ou l'Ambition Féminine au XVIIIe siècle* (Paris: Flammarion, 2006), p. 208.
[11] Rousseau, *Émile*, pp. 194–96.

From the beginning of the excerpt from *Émile* included here it is clear that Rousseau is confident he has already comprehensively proved that men and women are fundamentally different according to Nature's design. He goes on to demonstrate how these differences should be preserved and reinforced when educating women.

He first dismisses the common objection that men deliberately train women to be vain and superficial so that they may more easily dominate them. If vanity is a fault, the responsibility lies with their mothers, under whose tutelage they learn to be the way they are. He knows that women complain that they cannot get a proper education because there are no colleges for girls, but sidesteps this by claiming that boys' colleges are also inadequate.

He refuses to engage with those previous writers who had argued for women's rights or used historical examples to demonstrate that women were capable of equalling men in political and artistic activities, by saying that nothing is proved by quoting exceptions. These defenders of women are mocked as 'gallant partisans of the fair sex': the implication being that they cannot seriously believe what they say but are engaging in meaningless flattery.

A significant reference is made to 'masculine virtues'. It was a widespread belief, supported by numerous writers from the medieval period onwards, that the virtues of men and women were different. The most important characteristics of a good man were courage, prudence and magnanimity. (Prudence was defined not merely as caution but as the ability to exercise proper judgment.) A woman's essential virtues were modesty (which included not only sexual chastity but also a refusal to draw attention to herself in any way), obedience and thrift. Women were also expected to be timid. A self-confident woman who looked people in the eye was condemned as 'brazen' and warned that society would assume she was little better than a prostitute. This concept of gender-defined virtues was one to which Catharine Macaulay and Mary Wollstonecraft particularly objected, as we shall see from later texts.

To Rousseau, however, its truth was self-evident. If women try to assume masculine virtues, they will fall short, and at the same time will fail to achieve their own natural function as women. He therefore advises mothers not to 'try to turn your daughter into a good man in defiance of nature'.

As he had stated earlier in the book, women's special purpose is to please men. Having previously shown the boy Émile being taught to be self-reliant and to ignore the judgments of society if they do not accord with his own principles, Rousseau now emphasises that in the case of women the opposite is true. What matters is not what they think but what men think of them, since Nature had decreed that women should be 'at the mercy of men's judgment'. It follows that the purpose of a woman's education is to teach her the proper relationship with men.

One of the ways in which women please men is through their looks, and Rousseau states with approval that an interest in physical adornment is natural in women, as can be proved from little girls' interest in dressing their dolls. More severe moralists were to take a different view, castigating women for being interested in their physical appearance and the vagaries of fashion. In a later passage in *Émile*, Rousseau also praises women for 'coquetry': the flirtatious granting and withdrawal of favours which he considered to be one of those weapons nature had given women to make up for their physical weakness. Later women writers, particularly Mary Wollstonecraft, were driven to exasperation by this, considering it immoral to encourage women to be insincere and deceitful, but to Rousseau it was one of the greatest charms of the sexual game.

The passage we are likely to find the most shocking is the one in which Rousseau explains how girls should be trained in docility and obedience by constant restraint. Whatever a girl chooses to do, she should be forced to stop and do something else, in order to become accustomed to being thwarted. This will break her spirit sufficiently to enable her to suffer without complaint whatever her future husband may impose on her, however unjust it may be. Having previously denied that he intended to make women into slaves, Rousseau justifies this by explaining that it merely reinforces their already docile nature.

Rousseau seems content to allow women to act according to their instincts as long as these have been properly channelled, and even expresses sympathy with the idea that it would be best to leave them in profound ignorance of everything other than the duties of their sex, but he is aware that in the present corrupt state of society this would run the risk of their being seduced by immoral men. It will therefore be necessary to encourage them to some extent to cultivate the faculty of reason. This, however, makes him uneasy, since first he claims to be uncertain as to whether women are capable of solid reason, and secondly he worries that it may be incompatible with 'the simplicity that becomes their sex'. He is concerned that if women can reason, then they can argue or disagree, and risk turning into those literary ladies who had made him feel so uncomfortable in their Paris salons.

He resolves this by concluding that in fact women do not need reason: the necessary obedience and fidelity to their husbands will arise from their instinct, the 'inner voice' that comes from what is in any case their natural inclination. He also observes that women are incapable of applying reason to anything other than basic practical tasks: the nature of their minds makes it impossible for them to generalise wider principles from observation. The combination of simple into complex ideas that John Locke had described as a human characteristic was, according to Rousseau, specific to the male sex.

In case any women should feel despondent over their intellectual inferiority,

Rousseau concludes by describing their compensating qualities. Through close observation of the men in authority over her, a woman can learn how to influence them with a subtle charm. He concedes that women have more wit — that is, instinctive knowledge — while men have more genius, meaning the ability to analyse and systematise ideas. Through their complementary attributes, they can create the harmonious whole that Nature intended.

❖

Jean-Jacques Rousseau
Émile, ou de l'Éducation
The Hague: Jean Néaulme, 1762

Once it has been proved that men and women are not and should not be of the same constitution either in character or temperament, it follows that they should not have the same education. In following the directions of Nature they should act in concert but they should not do the same things; their labours have the same end but their tasks are different, and consequently the tastes which guide them are different also. We have tried to train up the natural man, and so as not to leave our task incomplete, let us consider how to train a woman fit to be his partner.

Do you wish to choose the right path at all times? Then always follow the directions of Nature. Everything that is characteristic of women should be respected as Nature's choice. You constantly say that women have certain faults that we do not have, but your vanity leads you astray: what would be a fault in you is a virtue in them, and things would not go so well if they did not have them. You must prevent these so-called defects from turning to the bad, but be careful not to eliminate them.

Women, for their part, never cease to complain that we bring them up to be vain and coquettish, and keep them amused by childish activities so we may more easily remain their masters; they blame us for the faults for which we reproach them. What folly! Since when did men meddle with girls' education? What prevents their mothers from bringing them up in any way they choose? Do they have no schools to go to? What a shame! I wish to God there were no boys' schools either: their education would be more sensible and virtuous. Do we force your daughters to waste their time on trivia? Do we compel them to spend half their lives in front of the mirror, as you do? Do we prevent you from instructing them, or having them instructed, in the way you wish? Is it our fault if they please us by their beauty, if we are fascinated by their airs and graces, and attracted and flattered by the arts you teach them; if we love to see them elegantly dressed; if we leave them to sharpen at their leisure the weapons with which they subjugate us? Go ahead and educate them like men, and the men will happily consent, for the more women wish to resemble them, the less they will be able to govern them — and then men will truly be the masters.

The faculties that are common to both sexes are not equally distributed, but overall they complement each other; woman is worth more as a woman and less as a man; whenever she asserts her rights she has the advantage over us; but when she tries to usurp ours she remains our inferior. No one can deny this general truth except by quoting exceptions, in the usual style of the gallant partisans of the fair sex.

If we cultivate masculine qualities in women and neglect those particular to them, we clearly act against their interest. Astute women see this too well to be taken in: in trying to usurp our privileges they never relinquish their own, but since they cannot reconcile these incompatible approaches, they fall short of their own standards while failing to reach ours, and thus lose half their value. Believe me, O wise mother, do not try to turn your daughter into a good man in defiance of nature; make her into an honest woman, and you can be sure that it will be better both for her and for us.

Does it follow that she should be raised in ignorance and restricted to domestic tasks? Will man make a servant of his companion, and deprive himself in her presence of the greatest charm of society? Will he prevent her from thinking and feeling, the better to subjugate her? Will he turn her into a mere machine? Certainly not: this is not what Nature intends by giving women such a pleasant and relaxing manner; on the contrary, Nature wishes them to think, to judge, to love and to know, to cultivate their minds as they do their figures; these are the weapons it gives them to compensate their weakness and manipulate our strength. Women should learn many things, but solely those that it is appropriate for them to know.

Whether I consider the particular destiny of the female sex, observe their inclinations or enumerate their duties, everything combines to indicate the type of education suitable to them. Woman and man are made for one another but their mutual dependence is not the same: men depend on women because of their desires; women depend on men because of their desires but also because of their needs. We would survive without them far better than they would without us. To supply their needs and fulfil their role, they rely on us to provide for them and to want to do so, and to consider them deserving of our support. They are dependent on our feelings, on the value we put on their merits, on our estimate of their charms and virtues. By the law of Nature women are, for themselves and for their children, at the mercy of men's judgment. It is not enough for them to be admirable, they must be admired; it is not enough for them to be beautiful, they must please; it is not enough for them to be good, they must be respected for it. Their honour does not consist only in their behaviour but in their reputation, and no woman who permits herself to lose her good name can ever be truly virtuous. A man of good conduct relies on himself alone and may defy public opinion, but if a woman acts well she has completed only half of her task, for what people think of her matters no less than what she really is. It follows that her system of education should, in this sense, be the opposite of ours: public opinion is the tomb of man's virtue but the throne of woman's.

The good constitution of children depends in the first case on that of their mother; the primary education of men depends on the women who care for them; women influence their manners, their passions, their tastes, their pleasures — in short, their happiness. Therefore the whole education of women should be conducted in relation to men. To please them, be useful to them, to make themselves loved and honoured by them; to raise them when young, to care for them when grown, to advise, console, make their lives sweet and pleasant: these are the duties of women for all time, and this is what they should be taught from their earliest childhood. The more we fail to respect this principle the more we shall miss the mark, and all the precepts we give them will do nothing for their happiness or for ours. [...]

Whatever jokers may say, common sense is found in equal measure in both sexes. Girls are in general more docile than boys, and it is necessary to treat them with more authority, as I shall soon explain, but it does not follow that we should expect them to do things whose use they do not understand. The mother's art is to show the relevance of everything they prescribe for them, and this is all the easier since girls' intelligence is more precocious than boys'. This rule excludes their sex as well as ours not only from useless studies that achieve nothing and do not even make their students more agreeable to others, but also from those that are beyond their ability at that age and whose future utility they cannot foresee. If I object to pushing a boy to learn to read, how much more do I object to forcing girls before they are made to understand the purpose of reading; the way we usually try to explain it accords with our ideas rather than theirs. After all, why does a little girl need to know how to read and write? Will she have a household to manage at such an early age? Most of them will abuse rather than use this fatal science, and they are all too curious to fail to learn it without compulsion, when they have the time and opportunity. Perhaps we should teach them numbers first of all, since nothing is more universally useful, needs longer practice or leaves less room for error than accounts. If our little girl will not get cherries for her tea without an arithmetical calculation, I can assure you she will learn to count soon enough. [...]

For the same reason that they have, or should have, little freedom, they carry to excess what little they have: they take everything to extremes, throwing themselves into their games with even more abandon than boys, which is the second problem I mentioned before. Their enthusiasm needs to be restrained, for it is the cause of several vices peculiar to women, such as caprice and obsession, by which a woman is in raptures today over something she will have forgotten tomorrow. The inconstancy of their desires is as dangerous as their excess, and both arise from the same source. Do not deprive them of noise, gaiety, laughter and silly games, but prevent them from growing bored with one before they move on to another; never suffer them to spend a single moment of their lives without the awareness of restraint. Accustom them to be interrupted in the middle of a game and returned to other tasks without complaint. You need nothing more than habit to achieve this, since it will reinforce their nature.

The result of this habitual constraint will be a docility that women will need throughout their lives, for they will never cease to be subordinate to a man, and to the opinions of all men, and they are never permitted to set themselves above these judgments. The first and most important quality in a woman is gentleness: since she is created to obey a creature as imperfect as man, who is often full of vice and always full of faults, she must learn at an early age to suffer even injustice, and to tolerate her husband's wrongs without complaint. It is not for his sake but for hers that she should be tender: spite and obstinacy in women never achieve anything other than to increase their suffering and their husbands' bad behaviour, for men are conscious that it is not with such weapons that their wives should vanquish them. Heaven has not made them manipulative and persuasive so they may become cantankerous; it has not made them weak to become domineering; it has not given them a soft voice to spout abuse, or delicate features to be distorted by anger. When they lose their temper they forget themselves: they may often have reason for complaint but they are always wrong to scold. Everyone should maintain the tone appropriate to their sex: a husband who is too mild can make an impertinent wife, but unless a man is a true monster, his wife's gentleness reforms him, and will triumph over him sooner or later. [...]

The whole human race is subject to a law that is more important than public opinion. All other laws should be subordinated to this inflexible direction: it is even the judge of prejudice, and it is only if public esteem is consistent with it that we should regard such esteem as having any authority.

This law is our individual conscience. I will not repeat what has already been said, but merely note that the education of women will always be defective if these two laws do not coincide. Conscience without concern for reputation will never give them the delicacy of soul that adorns good actions with worldly praise, while concern for opinion without conscience will always make women false and dishonest, valuing appearance above true virtue.

They must therefore cultivate a faculty that will create a balance between these two guides, which will not let their conscience go astray but will correct the errors of prejudice. This faculty is reason — but how many questions are suggested by this word! Are women capable of solid reasoning? Is it important for them to cultivate it? Can they cultivate it with success? Can this culture be applied to the functions incumbent upon them; is it compatible with the simplicity that becomes their sex?

The various ways of imagining and resolving these questions fall into two opposite extremes: one keeps women at home sewing and spinning with their maids and makes them into nothing more than the chief servant of their master, and the other is not content to secure their rights but makes them usurp our own; for to make women superior to us in the virtues specific to their sex and equal to us in the virtues common to both, what is this but to transfer to the wife the pre-eminence that Nature has given to the husband?

The reason that teaches man his duties is not complex, and the reason that teaches women theirs is even simpler. The obedience and fidelity she owes to her husband, the tender care she owes to her children, these are such natural and obvious consequences of her condition that she cannot honestly refuse her consent to the inner sense that guides her, nor fail to understand the duty inherent in an inclination that has never been perverted to this day.

I would not entirely reject the view that a woman should be restricted to the tasks proper to her sex and left in profound ignorance of everything else; but this would succeed only if public morality were simple and wholesome, or else require her to live in strict seclusion. In large towns and in a corrupt society such a woman would be too easy to seduce: her virtue would often be at the mercy of circumstances, and in this philosophical[12] age it must be strong enough to resist temptation. She needs to know in advance what a man might propose to her, and how she should react. [...]

Research into abstract and speculative truths, the principles and axioms of science, everything that tends towards the generalisation of ideas, these are not the sphere of women. Their studies should be entirely practical; it is for them to apply the principles men have propounded, and to make the observations on which men will base their principles. All of women's thoughts that are not immediately connected with their duties should focus on the study of men or on those agreeable subjects that help to form good taste, for works of genius are beyond their capacity, and they do not have sufficient accuracy or attention to succeed in the exact sciences. As for the physical sciences, it is for the sex that is the most active and outgoing, which sees furthest, has the greatest strength and exercises it most, to judge the relationship between living beings and the laws of nature. Woman, who is feeble and whose horizons are limited, weighs and judges the forces she can use to compensate for her weakness — these forces are the passions of men. The mechanism she uses is even stronger than ours, for her levers may move the human heart. She must acquire the art of making

---

[12] In France, the opponents of contemporary philosophers accused them of promoting immorality.

us desire those things that her sex cannot achieve on its own and which she finds necessary or agreeable. She must therefore study in depth the mind of man: not man in the abstract but the men who surround her, the men to whom she is subordinate either by law or by custom. She must learn to penetrate their feelings through their speech, their actions, their looks and their gestures. And by her own speech, looks and gestures, she must learn to inspire in them the emotions that please her, without even appearing to try. Men may philosophise about the human heart, but she will read far better into the hearts of men. It is, in a sense, for women to discover experimental morality, and for us to reduce it to a system. Woman has more wit and man more genius; woman observes and man reasons: this combination results in the clearest understanding and the most complete learning that the human mind is able to acquire; in a word, the most certain knowledge of ourselves and others of which our race is capable; and this is how art can be a constant aid in perfecting the instrument given to us by Nature.

— 2 —
James Fordyce

James Fordyce (1720–1796) was a Scottish minister and popular society preacher who was appointed in 1760 to the Presbyterian church on Monkwell Street in London. He was young, tall and handsome, with a fine speaking voice, and drew large crowds to his sermons. He preached on moral rather than theological topics, and saw it as his responsibility to improve the behaviour of his genteel and respectable audience.

One of Fordyce's favourite topics was advice to the young women in his congregation, and in 1766 he took the opportunity to publish a collection of these as *Sermons for Young Women*.[1] Fordyce's style is very different from Rousseau's: this is a work not of philosophical speculation but of practical advice as to how women should behave in society and attract husbands. It is their outward behaviour rather than their fundamental nature that concerns him. However, it will become clear that the views of the Swiss philosopher and the English cleric were very similar: Fordyce took it for granted that women were men's intellectual inferiors, and had been put on earth to carry out different functions.

He starts his sermon by warning his audience that men who are looking for a wife are not attracted to 'witty females'. The eighteenth-century use of the word 'wit' included shades of meaning that are hard to capture today: in the case of a woman, it was understood that she was clever, but displayed her cleverness in an inappropriately ostentatious manner.[2] What is more, if she did not agree with the men around her, she would say so and thus become a critic — and as Fordyce declares, what man would want a critic in his own household?

Even worse is the woman who is not as clever as she thinks she is, and therefore displays only 'the affectation of wit'. She will be despised as conceited and 'impertinent', a word that denoted someone or something that was

---

[1] James Fordyce, *Sermons for Young Women* (London: D. Payne, 1766).
[2] The word 'clever' was not commonly used at the time; Johnson's Dictionary in 1755 said 'This is a low word, scarcely every used but in burlesque or conversation'. The appropriate term for a man was 'ingenious', but this tended not to be applied to women. 'Understanding' was used to denote mental capacity, 'intelligence' generally meant information rather than mental ability, and 'intellectual' as applied to a person dates only from the twentieth century.

inappropriate or out of place. Women who do have knowledge should be careful not to show it: Fordyce quotes a poem by Edward Young to the effect that women should not display their mental abilities, but leave them for men to discover.

Fordyce reassures us that he does not expect women to keep silent at all times (as had been advocated by moralists of earlier periods), but admonishes mothers to take steps at an early stage to suppress their daughters' talkativeness. The only thing worse than one 'female tongue let loose into boundless loquacity' is a whole group of women all talking at once. They should realise that such a thing is impossible for a man to bear.

Fordyce is advocating a happy medium, and we may sympathise with criticism of inane chatter or impolite interruption, but of course it is difficult to know where he would draw the line: he does not specify how he would distinguish between 'laudable inquisitiveness' and 'improper curiosity'.

Fordyce does not fulminate against learned ladies as being contrary to nature, but is concerned that such women will lose their natural 'softness'. This is one of his favourite words in relation to women, and appears repeatedly throughout the two volumes of his *Sermons*. He frequently encouraged women to display helplessness, so as to encourage men to come chivalrously to their aid. (Mary Wollstonecraft was to find this profoundly irritating.)

The purpose of female education is to inculcate four qualities: 'sobriety, usefulness, self-enjoyment and the powers of pleasing'. It will teach women to be well-behaved, and capable of entertaining their husbands and whiling away the hours of solitude. Their usefulness will be displayed within the domestic rather than the public sphere.

Fordyce tackles the question of which intellectual (rather than elegant) improvements are appropriate to women. He repeats the assumptions that were by his time widely accepted, that women's brains are weak like their bodies, and that they are not capable of abstract thought. Like Rousseau, he informs women that 'your business is chiefly to read men', an exercise that requires 'observation and discernment', not 'reasoning or accuracy'. He is also aligned with Rousseau in insisting that it is in women's own interests that they should leave intellectual pursuits to men and concentrate on influencing men through their emotions. Women are not to resent this inferiority, since it is God himself that has put men and women in separate spheres, in which 'excellence' is differently defined.

As much as Rousseau, Fordyce is determined to see off the argument that women have suffered at the hands of men by being deliberately kept in a state of ignorance. He refutes this utterly and puts the blame back on women. There is nothing to stop them improving themselves, he insists, by spending their time and money on useful pursuits instead of their usual trivial obsessions.

Fordyce concludes with an extended mockery of the female pedant. Pedantry was an accusation that was regularly levelled at learned ladies; it implied that their learning was only partial and superficial, and that they insisted on showing off what information they had picked up even though — or perhaps because — they did not fully understand it. But Fordyce is happy to reassure his audience that learned ladies are a rare breed, and it is unlikely any of his audience will ever come across one of these curious creatures.

Fordyce's *Sermons* was immensely popular: it went through six editions in the first year of publication and was regularly reprinted throughout the century, as well as being translated into several European languages. It was for a long time one of the most popular books for well-intentioned friends or relatives to give to young ladies, though whether they read it assiduously, or indeed took much notice of what it said, may be questioned. In his play *The Rivals*,[3] Sheridan portrays his empty-headed heroine Lydia Languish, on hearing her guardian Mrs Malaprop coming up the stairs, hastily throwing the novels she has been reading into the closet and laying a copy of Fordyce's *Sermons* on the table. The book also appears in Jane Austen's *Pride & Prejudice*,[4] in which Mr Bennet mischievously asks his dull and pompous guest Mr Collins to read from it to the family after dinner, causing the flighty Lydia to interrupt him rudely. The ubiquity of the *Sermons* meant Austen had no need to describe what Mr Collins was reading, since all her readers would have appreciated the joke.

❖

James Fordyce
Sermons for Young Women
Dublin: W. Johnston, 1766 (3rd edition)

Sermon v. On Female Virtue, Friendship and Conversation

But when I speak on this subject, need I tell you, that men of the best sense have been usually averse to the thought of marrying a witty female? You will probably tell me they were afraid of being outshone; and some of them perhaps might be so. But I am apt to believe that many of them acted on different motives. Men who understand the science of domestic happiness know that its very first principle is ease. Of that indeed we grow fonder, in whatever condition, as we advance in life and as the heat of youth abates. But we cannot be easy where we are not safe. We are never safe in the company of a critic; and almost every wit is a critic by profession. In such company we are not at liberty to unbend ourselves. All must be the straining of study, or the anxiety

---

[3] Richard Sheridan, *The Rivals* (London: John Wilkie, 1775).
[4] Jane Austen, *Pride & Prejudice* (London: T. Egerton, 1813). The book was written in 1796.

of apprehension: how painful! Where the heart may not expand and open itself with freedom, farewell to real friendship, farewell to convivial delight! But to suffer this restraint at home, what misery! From the brandishings of wit in the hand of ill-nature, or imperious passion, or of unbounded vanity, who would not flee? But when that weapon is pointed at a husband, is it to be wondered if from his own house he take shelter in the tavern?

He sought a soft friend; he expected to be happy in a reasonable companion. He has found a perpetual satirist, or a self-sufficient prattler. How have I pitied such a man, when I have seen him in continual fear on his own account and that of his friends, and for the poor lady herself; lest in the run of her discourse, she should be guilty of some petulance, or some indiscretion, that would expose her and hurt them all! But take the matter at the best; there is still all the difference in the world between the entertainer of an evening, and a partner for life. Of the latter a sober mind, steady attachment and gentle manners, joined to a good understanding, will ever be the chief recommendations; whereas the qualities that sparkle will be often sufficient for the former.

As to the affectation of wit, one can hardly say whether it be most ridiculous or hurtful. The abuse of it, which we have been just considering, we are sometimes, perhaps too often, inclined to forgive, for the sake of that amusement which in spite of all the improprieties mentioned it yet affords. The other is universally contemptible and odious. Who is not shocked by the flippant impertinence of a self-conceited woman, that wants to dazzle by the supposed superiority of her powers? If you, my fair ones, have knowledge and capacity, let it be seen, by your not affecting to show them, that you have something much more valuable, humility and wisdom.

> Naked in nothing should a woman be,
> But veil her very wit with modesty.
> Let man discover, let not her display,
> But yield her charms of mind with sweet delay.[5]

Must women then keep silence in the house, as well as in the church? By no means. There may indeed be many cases in which it will particularly become a young lady to observe the apostolic rule, 'Be swift to hear and slow to speak',[6] but there are many too, wherein it will be no less fit that with an unassuming air she should endeavour to support and enliven the conversation. It is the opinion of some that girls should never speak before company, when their parents are present; and parents there are, so deficient in understanding as to make this a rule. How then shall those girls learn to acquit themselves properly in their absence? It is hard if you cannot distinguish, and teach your daughters to distinguish, between good breeding and pertness, between an obliging study

[5] Edward Young (1683–1765), *The Love of Fame, a Universal Passion*, Satire 6, 1728.
[6] The Biblical text is from 1 James 1. 19.

to please and an indecent desire to put themselves forward, between a laudable inquisitiveness and an improper curiosity. But this, I confess, is not the most common mistake in the education of young women; and they must permit me to say that it were well if the generality of mothers were careful, by prudent instruction in private, to repress that talkative humour which runs away with so many of them, and never quits them all their life after, for want of being curbed in their early years. But what words can express the impertinence of a female tongue let loose into boundless loquacity? Nothing can be more stunning, except where a number of Fine Ladies open at once. Protect us, ye powers of gentleness and decorum, protect us from the disgust of such a scene. Ah! my dear hearers, if ye knew how terrible it appears to a male ear of the least delicacy, I think you would take care never to practise it. [...]

For my part, I could heartily wish to see the female world more accomplished than it is; but I do not wish to see it abound with metaphysicians, historians, speculative philosophers, or learned Ladies of any kind. I should be afraid, lest the sex should lose in softness what they gained in force; and lest the pursuit of such elevation should interfere a little with the plain duties and humble virtues of life.

Amiable instances of the contrary I know there are. I think at this moment of one lady, in particular, who, to an extensive knowledge in philosophy and languages ancient and modern, with some portion of poetical genius, and a considerable degree of literary fame, has the sense and worth to join every domestic quality that can adorn a woman in her situation.[7]

To inculcate such qualities, together with those elegant and intellectual improvements which young ladies would do well to acquire, with a view to sobriety, usefulness, self-enjoyment, and the powers of pleasing, will be the business of some subsequent addresses. [...]

Sermon VII. On Female Virtue, with Intellectual Accomplishments

The degree of those Intellectual Accomplishments which your sex should aim at, I pretend not to determine. That must depend on the capacities, opportunities and encouragements which you severally enjoy. With regard to all these, however, this may be said in general, that they are better and more than many of you seem solicitous to improve.

As to the first indeed, I scruple not to declare my opinion that Nature appears to have formed the faculties of your sex for the most part with less vigour than those of ours; observing the same distinction here as in the more delicate frame of your bodies. Exceptions we readily admit, and such as do the individuals

---

[7] This probably refers to Elizabeth Carter (1717–1806), renowned as a Classicist but also as modest and pious.

great honour in those particular walks of excellence wherein they have been distinguished. But you yourselves, I think, will allow that war, commerce, politics, exercises of strength and dexterity, abstract philosophy, and all the abstruser sciences, are most properly the province of men. I am sure those masculine women that would plead for your sharing any part of this province equally with us, do not understand your true interests. There is an influence, there is an empire which belongs to you, and which I wish you ever to possess: I mean that which has the heart for its object, and is secured by meekness and modesty, by soft attraction and virtuous love.

But now I must add that your powers in this way will receive a large accession from the culture of your minds, in the more elegant and polished branches of knowledge. When I say so, I would by no means insinuate that you are not capable of the judicious and the solid, in such proportion as is suited to your destination in life. This, I apprehend, does not require reasoning or accuracy so much as observation and discernment. Your business chiefly is to read Men, in order to make yourselves agreeable and useful. It is not the argumentative but the sentimental talents, which give you that insight and those openings into the human heart that lead to your principal ends as women. Nevertheless, in this study you may derive great assistance from books. Without them, in effect, your progress here will be partial and confined. Neither are you to attach yourselves wholly to this study, important as it is, and grateful as you may find it. Whatever kinds of reading may contribute to your general improvement and satisfaction, as reasonable beings designed for society, virtue and religion, will deserve your attentive regard. [...]

Of this I am certain, that amongst women of sense I have discovered an uncommon penetration in what relates to characters, an uncommon dexterity in hitting them off through their several specific distinctions, and even nicer discriminations, together with a race of fancy and a fund of what may be strictly termed Sentiment, or a pathetic manner of thinking, which I have not so frequently met with in men. It should seem that Nature, by her liberality to the female mind in these respects, has seen fit to compensate what has been judged a defect in point of depth and force; and a real defect I believe it is, if estimated absolutely. If estimated with a due regard to the design and formation of the sex, it ought to be considered as no defect at all.

I have already hinted that to men and women the Almighty has allotted very different provinces, on the filling of which with suitable kinds of ability and excellence depends, under his conduct, the proper perfection and welfare of each. In all I have said therefore, or may yet say, concerning Female Accomplishments, I would be still understood as recommending what is refined in study, and useful in the milder modes of life; not what is profound in the former, or of no material advantage in the latter.

This hinders not however, but that those ladies whom Nature, not confining herself to her customary operations, has endowed with any signal strength of genius, may, if favoured also by their situation, give way to that original bent, by prosecuting severer studies to every prudent length. I say, to every prudent length. For should they push their application so far as to hurt their more tender health, to hinder those family duties for which the sex are chiefly intended, or to impair those softer graces that give them their highest lustre; nothing, I think, can be more apparent than that, in such cases, they would relinquish their just sphere, for one much less amiable, and much less beneficial. [...]

But I think I hear you exclaiming that, though God has given you the capacities of intellectual improvement, men have denied you the opportunities of it. Let us therefore proceed to examine how this matter stands, which was our second point. If your complaint be well-founded, you are certainly objects of pity instead of blame. If the men, jealous of dominion, do really seek to depress the women by keeping them in a state of ignorance, they are surely guilty of equal cruelty and meanness. But though the complaint be a very common one, and very popular with your sex, I must take the liberty of saying that it appears to me without any foundation adequate to the bitterness with which it has been made, or to the keenness with which it has been propagated.

That your minds are often much neglected at home, that they are neglected perhaps yet more at many Boarding-schools, we readily admit and heartily regret. But are you nevertheless desirous of knowledge? Then what should hinder you from attaining it? Is there any law or statute by which you are prohibited, under severe pains and penalties, to read or to think if you be so minded? Books you have, or may have, on every subject that is proper for you. This is not a country where these are scarce; where friendship, if permitted, will not supply, or where benevolence, if asked, will not lend them. You will be pleased to remember too that the price of one expensive gown or of one shining toy, will at any time furnish a little library of the best authors. Nor does it appear that you are at a loss to find as many plays and novels as the most insatiable avidity can devour. But in fact there are few young ladies who are not tolerably provided with books useful as well as amusing; and in those who are not under the necessity of earning their bread, it is both an idle and unthankful pretence, to plead that they want either opportunity or leisure for any one study befitting their sex.

Not to speak of the time that with so much propriety they might, and that for so many reasons, they ought to redeem from endless visitings and other follies; what is there to prevent their reading alternately to one another, when custom or convenience engages them at work together?[8] Such an exercise would not only enlarge the stock of ideas in each individual, but also present materials

---

[8] 'Work' meant needlework.

on which their minds might operate, with an energy quickened by mutual exertion [...] How smoothly have I seen those hours steal away which were thus employed in a little ring of intelligent females, all sweetly solicitous to improve and be improved by each other! [...]

Besides the little opportunities of mental culture now enumerated, I must not forget to add that in all probability there are few young ladies who are not, or who may not be, acquainted with some persons of both sexes, endowed alike with worth and capacity, that would take the highest pleasure, by their conversation and counsel, to aid them in the pursuit of knowledge. Which brings me to consider, in the last place, your complaints of want of encouragement to that pursuit. Who are they then that seek to discourage you? I have read of foolish mothers, that would not suffer their daughters to read, lest they should dim the lustre of their eyes, or spoil the bloom of their complexions. But I have never met with one that seriously carried her folly so far. On the other hand, I have known parents not a few who, though they had little or no taste for knowledge themselves, would yet speak with the utmost satisfaction of a girl that was fond of her books.

But perhaps my little friend is afraid, lest the men should suspect her of being what the world styles in derision a Learned Lady. Indeed? Is this then a character so very easily acquired, that you are in danger of it the moment you emerge from the depth of ignorance, and begin to think and speak like a reasonable being? You are over hasty in your apprehension. A learned lady is by no means a creature that we run the risk of being often shocked with. For my own part, I have never strictly speaking seen such a one; and when at any time I have met with what approached to that character, I must profess I found nothing to excite terror. But possibly you mean a smatterer[9] in learning. There indeed I join with you in wishing you may never incur the imputation.

That men are frighted at Female pedantry, is very certain. A woman that affects to dispute, to decide, to dictate on every subject; that watches or makes opportunities of throwing out scraps of literature, or shreds of philosophy, in every company; that engrosses the conversation, as if she alone were qualified to entertain; that betrays, in short, a boundless intemperance of tongue, together with an inextinguishable passion for shining by the splendour of her supposed talents; such a woman is truly insufferable. At first, perhaps, she may be considered merely as an object of ridicule; but she soon grows into an object of aversion. Be assured however that, where a character so unnatural appears, it is not the effect of too much knowledge, but of too little. The deep river flows on

---

[9] A smatterer was a person who had pretensions to learning but was in practice only superficially knowledgeable. Fanny Burney (1752–1840), in her unpublished play *The Witlings*, had a character called Lady Smatter who is generally assumed to be a caricature of Elizabeth Montagu (1718–1800). Hannah More uses the same term in the text included in this volume.

with a noble stillness, while the shallow stream runs babbling along. Suspicious of her own deficiency, the Pedant we describe suspects lest you should discover it; but instead of learning caution from that consciousness, she strives to dazzle you with the little she does know. Or else, what is more probable, elated with that which to her circumscribed view appears great, she cannot restrain herself from displaying it on all occasions; when farther progress, and higher ground, would have taught her modesty, by[10] showing her immense regions of truth yet untravelled, of which she had no conception before.

[10] The text says 'but'.

— 3 —
Hester Chapone

Hester Mulso (1727–1801) was the daughter of a Northamptonshire country gentleman, and the only girl in a family with four sons. She was obviously clever: she read through the novels in her father's library, and apparently penned her first romance at the age of nine. However, Hester's mother did not approve of educating girls, and it was not until she died in 1750, when Hester was already twenty-three, that she felt free to follow her own wishes. She became fluent in French and Italian and also taught herself Latin. She entered into a prolonged correspondence with the famous novelist Samuel Richardson, and wrote poetry and plays.

Hester wished to marry her neighbour John Chapone, a lawyer, but her father forbade the match, and they endured a six-year engagement until he finally relented. Unfortunately, the marriage was as short as the engagement had been long, and her husband died after ten months, leaving her in difficult financial circumstances; she never remarried.

Chapone became a friend of Elizabeth Carter (1717–1806), the daughter of a Kent clergyman who had taught her Latin and Greek, subjects which were generally regarded as unsuitable for women. Carter became a renowned Classicist, and in 1758 published the first English translation of the works of the Greek philosopher Epictetus;[1] the British, who had become jealous of French women's superiority in literature, adopted her as their very own learned lady. Her intellectual ability was made acceptable by her modesty and piety, and by the fact that she never married.

Chapone and Carter were members of the bluestocking circle led by Elizabeth Montagu (1718–1800). This was modelled on the French salons, where women presided over meetings of mixed company in their own homes, and it attracted such luminaries as Dr Samuel Johnson, the playwright Richard Sheridan and the artist Sir Joshua Reynolds. Montagu herself published a book on Shakespeare,[2] rejecting the criticisms of the national bard made by

[1] Elizabeth Carter, *All the Works of Epictetus that are now Extant* (London: S. Richardson, A. Millar, J. Rivington and R. & J. Dodsley, 1758).
[2] Elizabeth Montagu, *An Essay on the Writings and Genius of Shakespear, compared with the Greek and French Dramatic Poets, with Some Remarks upon the Misrepresentations of Mons. De Voltaire* (London: J. Dodsley, Baker & Leigh, J. Walter, T. Cadell, J. Wilkie, 1769).

Voltaire. These women were anxious to ensure that intellectual women did not suffer the same attacks as their French counterparts: they insisted that their assemblies should be free of alcohol, gambling and gallantry, and were staunch supporters of the established Church of England. Conscious of the suspicion that learned ladies were slovenly pedants who neglected their families, they wished to demonstrate that women could be at once learned, respectable and sociable. Since Montagu, Carter and Chapone were all childless, the domestic ideal propounded by Rousseau did not represent a solution to their individual ambitions.

In 1773 Hester Chapone published a book entitled *Letters on the Improvement of the Mind*,[3] addressed to her fifteen-year-old niece and dedicated to Elizabeth Montagu. It fitted into one of the most popular literary genres in England during the late eighteenth century: the conduct book. These instruction manuals on the correct way to behave came in all sorts of forms — sermons, letters and essays — and were written by both men and women. Some were highly religious, while others were little more than manuals of etiquette.

Chapone's book was wildly popular: the first edition of 1500 copies sold out rapidly and a second edition appeared in the same year. By 1829 it had been reprinted nearly thirty times and translated into French. In *A Vindication of the Rights of Woman*,[4] Mary Wollstonecraft singled it out as one of the few conduct books that deserved praise. Unfortunately, Chapone did not benefit from this success, since she had sold the copyright to the original publisher for the modest sum of £50.

Where Rousseau stated that the purpose of women's education was to teach them to please men, Chapone insisted that its objective was to prepare them for the life to come: their task is 'no less than to bring your frail nature to that degree of Christian perfection, which is to qualify it for immortality'. To a devout Christian, Rousseau's claim that children were born innocent and only corrupted by society was quite wrong, for the Bible taught that all are born with the taint of original sin. Nevertheless, their educational programmes both aimed to correct the faults to which they believed women were naturally prone, and to put them on the path of virtue. Her niece must correct and purify her heart, form and govern her temper and manners, and qualify herself as a useful and agreeable member of society.

Since religion is all-important, Chapone instructs her niece to start by reading the Bible, where she will find 'all the truths necessary to be believed, and plain and easy directions for the practice of every duty'. She then moves on to moral subjects, warning against vanity, which she believes to be a universal

---

[3] Hester Chapone, *Letters on the Improvement of the Mind, Addressed to a Young Lady* (London: J. Walter, 1773).
[4] Mary Wollstonecraft, *A Vindication of the Rights of Woman* (London: J. Johnson, 1792).

female failing, and concluding that 'religion is indeed the only effectual remedy for this evil', since it inspires humility and prevents people from seeking 'the applause of men'. She does not approve of the fashion for extreme sensibility or the practice of teaching young women that 'tenderness and softness is the peculiar charm of the sex — that even their weakness is lovely, and their fears becoming'. This is contrary to the message of some conduct books written by men: Dr John Gregory (1724-1773), for instance, recommended the most extreme shyness and delicacy as appropriate for girls who wished to attract a husband: they should even conceal robust health and merriment behind a veil of helplessness.[5] (These sentiments were to rouse Mary Wollstonecraft to a pitch of exasperation.) Chapone insists that women are rational beings, and their natural feelings of compassion should lead not to wallowing in uncontrolled emotion but to positive action on behalf of others.

Chapone reminds her niece that a woman's virtues must be domestic: 'within the circle of her own family and dependants lies her sphere of action'. She gives practical advice about the running of a household: she needs to take charge of expenses, keep her house neat and tidy, make sure her servants are not cheating her, pay tradesmen on time, and keep enough aside to be able to make charitable donations to the poor.

As regards female 'accomplishments', Chapone makes the usual recommendations of learning good handwriting, basic arithmetic, French and Italian, dancing, music, and drawing. She does not advise the learned languages, and confirms the standard opinion with regard to deeper study: women should restrict themselves to works of the imagination and avoid anything that requires deep analytical thought, for a woman famed for her learning will be disliked by men and women alike.

Chapone does, however, expect her niece to be better educated than the norm, assuming that she will have read translations of Homer and Virgil, as well as Shakespeare and Milton. She sets out a structured and comprehensive course of reading in history and geography which she describes as a 'moderate scheme', but which would be severely testing to a modern fifteen-year-old. When it comes to the dangerous topic of fiction, Chapone is conventionally nervous, since novels tend to lead girls to expect a life full of adventures, and to be disappointed by the quiet domesticity they are more likely to experience.

The need to keep a balance between intellectual and social accomplishments was emphasised by Vicesimus Knox, the headmaster of Tonbridge School, who wrote an essay on female education in 1779 in the form of a letter from a young lady who has been brought up by her clergyman father, learned classical and European languages, and read extensively in Greek, Latin, French and Italian

---

[5] Dr John Gregory, *A Father's Legacy to His Daughters* (Edinburgh: Strahan, Cadell, Balfour & Creech, 1774).

literature, but has discovered to her alarm that other women are overawed by her, and men consider her too learned to be a satisfactory wife. Knox wished to reassure his readers that learning does not necessarily render a woman unwilling to fulfil the traditional female role, and gave the bluestockings as examples, albeit as exceptions to the norm:

> That learning belongs not to the female character, and that the female mind is not capable of a degree of improvement equal to that of the other sex, are narrow and unphilosophical prejudices. The present times exhibit most honourable instances of female learning and genius in a Montagu, a Chapone, and a Carter.[6]

Chapone did not mention Rousseau in her book; indeed, the bluestocking ladies disapproved of his works. Elizabeth Carter wrote to Elizabeth Montagu that *Julie* was 'one of the most dangerous and wicked books, in many respects, that I believe ever was published'.[7] She also disliked *Émile*, finding Rousseau to be a fine stylist, 'but with such a mixture of wrong principles and false reasoning, that renders him the most dangerous writer I ever read'.[8] Chapone later read Rousseau's posthumous works, in which he expressed his paranoid fear that the whole of Europe was conspiring against him: she found them to be 'most melancholy reading, as they show the most evident madness, and that of the most miserable and afflicting kind'.[9]

Chapone shared Rousseau's belief in the domestic destiny of the female sex, but differed strongly with him on the question of how women should be educated. Rousseau had recommended that girls be taught the outward practices of religion as a means of enforcing their submission to social norms: it did not even matter if they followed a false faith, for 'the docility which causes mother and daughter to submit to the order of nature will in God's eyes wipe out the sin of error'. Chapone, by contrast, insisted on a serious engagement with the scriptures as the basis of all morality. She also set out a broad programme of reading that would, if dutifully followed, give her niece a well-stocked mind and train her in independent thought, and justified this on the basis that it was a religious duty to 'cultivate the powers entrusted to us, and to render ourselves as perfect as we can'.

The *Letters* did not propound any philosophical theory of femininity, but were a practical approach to the education of a young gentlewoman which, if followed by an adept student, would make her well-informed as well as competent to run a household and educate her own children. The work did

---

[6] Vicesimus Knox, *Essays Moral and Literary* (London: E. & C. Dilly, 1779), p. 334.
[7] Letter to Elizabeth Montagu, 20 August 1774, *Letters from Mrs Elizabeth Carter to Mrs. Montagu, between the Years 1755 and 1800, Chiefly upon Literary and Moral Subjects*, ed. by Montagu Pennington, 3 vols (London: J. Rivington, 1817), II, p. 268.
[8] *Letters from Mrs Elizabeth Carter to Mrs Montagu*, II, p. 268.
[9] *The Posthumous Works of Mrs Chapone*, 2 vols (London: John Murray, 1807), I, p. 80.

not complain about the treatment of women or challenge social expectations, and it became a popular book for well-meaning relatives to give to young ladies. However, its religious tone and acceptance of social restraints made it something of a byword for dull conformity, and Chapone's *Letters* is one of the books that the rebellious Becky Sharp throws out of the carriage window as she escapes from school in Thackeray's *Vanity Fair*.[10]

❖

Hester Chapone
Letters on the Improvement of the Mind
London: J. Walters, 1773

Letter VIII — On Politeness and Accomplishments

Whilst you labour to enrich your mind with the essential virtues of Christianity — with piety, benevolence, meekness, humility, integrity, and purity — and to make yourself useful in domestic management, I would not have my dear child neglect to pursue those graces and acquirements, which may set her virtue in the most advantageous light, adorn her manners, and enlarge her understanding: and this, not in the spirit of vanity, but in the innocent and laudable view of rendering herself more useful and pleasing to her fellow-creatures, and consequently more acceptable to God. Politeness of behaviour, and the attainment of such branches of knowledge and such arts and accomplishments as are proper to your sex, capacity, and station, will prove so valuable to yourself through life, and will make you so desirable a companion, that the neglect of them may reasonably be deemed a neglect of duty; since it is undoubtedly our duty to cultivate the powers entrusted to us, and to render ourselves as perfect as we can. [...]

With regard to accomplishments, the chief of these is a competent share of reading, well chosen and properly regulated; and of this I shall speak more largely hereafter. Dancing and the knowledge of the French tongue are now so universal that they cannot be dispensed with in the education of a gentlewoman; and indeed they both are useful as well as ornamental; the first, by forming and strengthening the body and improving the carriage; the second, by opening a large field of entertainment and improvement for the mind. I believe there are more agreeable books of female literature in French than in any other language; and as they are not less commonly talked of than English books, you must often feel mortified in company, if you are too ignorant to read them. Italian would

---

[10] William Makepeace Thackeray, *Vanity Fair, a Novel without a Hero* (London: Punch Office, 1847).

be easily learned after French, and if you have leisure and opportunity, may be worth your gaining, though in your station of life it is by no means necessary.

To write a free and legible hand, and to understand common arithmetic, are indispensable requisites.

As to music and drawing, I would only wish you to follow as Genius[11] leads; you have some turn for the first, and I should be sorry to see you neglect a talent which will at least afford you an innocent amusement, though it should not enable you to give much pleasure to your friends. I think the use of both these arts is more for yourself than for others; it is but seldom that a private person has leisure or application enough to gain any high degree of excellence in them, and your own partial family are perhaps the only persons who would not much rather be entertained by the performance of a professor than by yours; but with regard to yourself, it is of great consequence to have the power of filling up agreeably those intervals of time which too often hang heavily on the hands of a woman, if her lot be cast in a retired situation.

Besides this, it is certain that even a small share of knowledge in these arts will heighten your pleasure in the performances of others: the taste must be improved before it can be susceptible of an exquisite relish for any of the imitative arts; an unskilful ear is seldom capable of comprehending *Harmony*, or of distinguishing the most *delicate* charms of *Melody*. The pleasure of seeing fine paintings, or even of contemplating the beauties of Nature, must be greatly heightened by our being conversant with the rules of drawing, and by the habit of considering the most picturesque objects. As I look upon taste to be an inestimable fund of innocent delight, I wish you to lose no opportunity of improving it, and of cultivating in yourself the relish of such pleasures as will not interfere with a rational scheme of life, nor lead you into dissipation, with all its attendant evils of vanity and luxury.

As to the learned languages, though I respect the abilities and application of those ladies who have attained them, and who make a modest and proper use of them, yet I would by no means advise you, or any other woman who is not strongly impelled by a particular genius, to engage in such studies. The labour and time which they require are generally incompatible with our natures and proper employments; the real knowledge which they supply is not essential, since the English, French or Italian tongues afford tolerable translations of all the most valuable productions of antiquity, besides the multitude of original authors which they furnish, and these are much more than sufficient to store your mind with as many ideas as you will know how to manage. The danger of pedantry and presumption in a woman — of her exciting envy in one sex and jealousy in the other — of her exchanging the graces of imagination for the

---

[11] In this context, 'genius' refers to a natural bent or inclination, and not necessarily to unusual excellence.

severity and preciseness of a scholar would be, I own, sufficient to frighten me from the ambition of seeing my girl remarkable for learning. Such objections are perhaps still stronger with regard to the abstruse sciences.

Whatever tends to embellish your fancy, to enlighten your understanding, and furnish you with ideas to reflect upon when alone, or to converse upon in company, is certainly well worth your acquisition. The wretched expedient to which ignorance often drives our sex, of calling in slander to enliven the tedious insipidity of conversation, would alone be a strong reason for enriching your mind with innocent subjects of entertainment, which may render you a fit companion for persons of sense and knowledge, from whom you may reap the most desirable improvements; for though I think reading indispensably necessary to the due cultivation of your mind, I prefer the conversation of such persons to every other method of instruction; but this you cannot hope to enjoy unless you qualify yourself to bear a part in such society by at least a moderate share of reading.

Though *religion* is the most important of all your pursuits, there are not many *books* on that subject which I should recommend to you at present. Controversy is wholly improper at your age, and it is also too soon for you to inquire into the evidence of the truth of revelation, or to study the difficult parts of scripture; when these shall come before you, there are many excellent books from which you may receive great assistance. At present, practical divinity — clear of superstition and enthusiasm,[12] but addressed to the heart, and written with a warmth and spirit capable of exciting in it a pure and rational piety — is what I wish you to meet with.

The principal study I would recommend is history. I know of nothing equally proper to entertain and improve at the same time, or that is so likely to form and strengthen your judgment, and by giving you a liberal and comprehensive view of human nature, in some measure to supply the defect of that experience which is usually attained too late to be of much service to us. Let me add that more materials for conversation are supplied by this kind of knowledge than by almost any other; but I have more to say to you on this subject in a future letter.

The faculty in which women usually most excel is that of imagination; and when properly cultivated, it becomes the source of all that is most charming in society. Nothing you can read will so much contribute to the improvement of the faculty as poetry, which if applied to its true ends, adds a thousand charms to those sentiments of religion, virtue, generosity and delicate tenderness, by which the human soul is exalted and refined. I hope you are not deficient in natural taste for this enchanting art, but that you will find it one of your

---

[12] Members of the Church of England used these terms to denote respectively Catholicism and Methodism, in the belief that Anglicanism pursued a moderate path between the two extremes.

greatest pleasures to be conversant with the best poets whom our language can bring you acquainted with, particularly those immortal ornaments of our nation, *Shakespeare* and *Milton*. The first is not only incomparably the noblest genius in dramatic poetry, but the greatest master of nature, and the most perfect characterizer of men and manners. In this last point of view, I think him inestimable, and I am persuaded that, in the course of your life, you will seldom find occasion to correct those observations on human nature, and those principles of morality, which you may extract from his capital pieces.

You will at first find his language difficult, but if you take the assistance of a friend who understands it well, you will be degrees enter into his manner of phraseology, and perceive a thousand beauties which at first lay buried in obsolete words and uncouth constructions. The admirable *Essay on Shakespeare*[13] which has lately appeared, so much to the honour of our sex, will open your mind to the peculiar excellencies of this author, and enlighten your judgment on dramatic poetry in general, with such force of reason and brilliancy of wit as cannot fail to delight as well as instruct you.

Our great English poet, Milton, is as far above my praise as his *Paradise Lost* is above anything which I am able to read, except the sacred writers. The sublimity of his subject sometimes leads him into abstruseness; but many parts of his great poem are easy to all comprehensions, and must find their way directly to every heart by the tenderness and delicacy of his sentiments, in which he is not less strikingly excellent than in the richness and sublimity of his imagination. Addison's criticism in the Spectators,[14] written with that beauty, elegance and judgment which distinguish all his writings, will assist you to understand and to relish this poem.

It is needless to recommend to you the translation of Homer and Virgil, which everybody reads that reads at all. You must have heard that Homer is esteemed the father of poetry, the original from whence all the moderns, not excepting Milton himself, borrow some of their greatest beauties, and from whom they extract those rules for composition which are found most agreeable to nature and true taste. Virgil, you know, is the next in rank among the classics: you will read his Eneid with extreme pleasure, if ever you are able to read Italian, in Annibal Caro's translation;[15] the idiom of the Latin and Italian languages being more alike, it is, I believe, much looser, yet preserves more the spirit of the original, than the English translations.

---

[13] *An Essay on the Writings and Genius of Shakespear* (1769) was written by Elizabeth Montagu, to whom Chapone dedicated the *Letters on the Improvement of the Mind*.

[14] Joseph Addison (1672–1719) was the editor of the *Spectator* magazine, which ran from 1711 to 1714; he wrote many of its articles himself, and was admired for his judgment and his style.

[15] This translation of Virgil's *Aeneid* was published as *L'Eneide di Virgilio* (Padua: Pietro Paolo Tozzi, 1613).

For the rest, fame will point out to you the most considerable of our poets, and I would not exclude any of name among those whose morality is unexceptionable; but of poets, as of all others, I wish you to read only such as are properly recommended to you, since there are many who debase their divine art by abusing it to the purposes of vice and impiety. If you could read poetry with a judicious friend, who would lead your judgment to a true discernment of its beauties and defects, it would inexpressibly heighten both your pleasure and improvement. But before you enter this, some acquaintance with the *Heathen Mythology* is necessary. I think that you must before now have met with some book under the title of *The Pantheon*, and if once you know as much of the gods and goddesses as the most common books on the subject will tell you, the rest may be learned by reading Homer; but then you must particularly attend to him in this view. I do not expect you to penetrate those numerous mysteries, those amazing depths of morality, religion and metaphysics which some pretend to have discovered in his mythology; but to know the names and principal offices of the gods and goddesses, with some idea of their moral meaning, seems requisite to the understanding almost any poetical composition.

As an instance of the moral meaning I speak of, I will mention an observation of Bossuet[16] that Homer's poetry was particularly recommended to the Greeks by the superiority which he ascribes to them over the Asiatics; this superiority is shown in the Iliad not only in the conquest of Asia by the Greeks, and in the actual destruction of its capital, but in the division and arrangement of the gods who took part with the contending nations. On the side of Asia was *Venus* — that is, sensual passion, pleasure and effeminacy. On the side of Greece was *Juno* — that is, matronly gravity and conjugal love; together *Mercury* — intention and eloquence; and *Jupiter*, or political wisdom. On the side of Asia was *Mars*, who represents brutal valour and blind fury. On that of Greece was *Pallas* — that is, military discipline and bravery, guarded by judgment.

This, and many other instances that might be produced will show you how much of the beauty of the poet's arts must be lost to you without some notion of these allegorical personages. Boys, in their school-learning, have this kind of knowledge impressed on their minds by a variety of books; but women, who do not go through the same course of instruction, are very apt to forget what little they read or hear on the subject. I advise you, therefore, never to lose an opportunity of inquiring into the meaning of anything you meet with in poetry or in painting, alluding to the history of any of the heathen deities, and of

---

[16] Jacques-Bénigne Bossuet (1627–1704), Bishop of Meaux, was a French theologian and controversialist. He issued numerous pamphlets which, together with his collected sermons, were published in thirty-one volumes after his death. He is a curious source for Chapone to use, since he was known for his strong opposition to Protestantism and support for the Revocation of the Edict of Nantes, which caused many French Protestants to flee to England and America.

obtaining from some friend an explanation of its connection with true history, or of its allegorical reference to morality or to physics.

Natural Philosophy,[17] in the largest sense of the expression, is too wide a field for you to undertake, but the study of nature, as far as may suit your powers and opportunities, you will find a most sublime entertainment: the objects of this study are all the stupendous works of the Almighty Hand that lie within the reach of our observation. In the works of man perfection is aimed at, but it can only be found in those of the Creator. The contemplation of perfection must produce delight, and every natural object around you would offer this delight, if it could attract your attention. If you survey the earth, every leaf that trembles in the breeze, every blade of grass beneath your feet, is a wonder as absolutely beyond the reach of human art to imitate as the construction of the universe. Endless pleasures to those who have a taste for them, might be derived from the endless variety to be found in the composition of this globe and its inhabitants. The fossil, the vegetable and the animal world, gradually rising in the scale of excellence; the innumerable species of each, still preserving their specific differences from age to age, yet of which no two individuals are ever perfectly alike, afford such a range for observation and inquiry as might engross the whole term of our short life if followed minutely. Besides all the animal creatures obvious to our unassisted senses, the eye aided by philosophical inventions sees myriads of creatures, which by the ignorant are not known to have existence. It sees all nature teem with life: every fluid — each part of every vegetable and animal — swarm with its peculiar inhabitants, invisible to the naked eye but as perfect in all their parts, and enjoying life as indisputable as the elephant or the whale.

But if from the earth, and from these minute wonders, the philosophic eye is raised towards the heavens, what a stupendous scene there opens to its view! Those brilliant lights that sparkle to the eye of ignorance as gems adorning the sky, or as lamps to guide the traveller by night, assume an importance that amazes the understanding — they appear to be *worlds*, formed like ours for a variety of inhabitants, or *suns*, enlightening numberless other worlds too distant for our discovery! I shall ever remember the astonishment and rapture with which my mind received this idea when I was about your age; it was then perfectly new to me, and it is impossible to describe the sensations I felt from the glorious, boundless prospect of infinite beneficence bursting at once upon my imagination! Who can contemplate such a scene unmoved? If our curiosity is excited to enter upon this noble inquiry, a few books on the subject, and those of the easiest sort, with some of the common experiments, may be sufficient for your purpose — which is to enlarge your mind and to excite in it the most ardent gratitude and profound adoration towards that great and good

---

[17] This term referred to what we now call 'science'.

Being who exerts his boundless power in communicating various portions of happiness through all the immense regions of creation.

Moral philosophy, as it relates to human actions, is of still higher importance than the study of nature. The works of the ancients on this subject are universally said to be entertaining as well as instructive, by those who can read them in their original languages; and such of them as are well translated will undoubtedly, some years hence, afford you great pleasure and improvement. You will also find many agreeable and useful books, written originally in French and in English, on morals and manners; for the present, there are works which, without assuming the solemn air of philosophy, will enlighten your mind on these subjects, and introduce instruction in an easier dress; of this sort are many of the moral essays that have appeared in periodical papers which, when excellent in their kind — as are the *Spectators, Guardians, Ramblers* and *Adventurers*[18] — are particularly useful to young people, as they comprehend a great variety of subjects, introduce many ideas and observations that are new to them, and lead to a habit of reflecting on the characters and events that come before them in real life, which I consider as the best exercise of the understanding.

Books on taste and criticism will hereafter be more proper for you than at present: whatever can improve your discernment and render your taste elegant and just, must be of great consequence to your enjoyments as well as to the embellishments of your understanding.

I would by no means exclude the kind of reading which young people are naturally most fond of, though I think the greatest care should be taken in the choice of those *fictitious stories* that so enchant the mind, most of which tend to inflame the passions of youth, whilst the chief purpose of education should be to moderate and restrain them. Add to this that both the writing and sentiments of most novels and romances are such as are only proper to vitiate your style, and mislead your heart and understanding. The expectation of extraordinary adventures, which seldom ever happen to the sober and prudent part of mankind, and the admiration of extravagant passions and absurd conduct, are some of the usual fruits of this kind of reading; which, when a young woman makes it her chief amusement, generally render her ridiculous in conversation, and miserably wrongheaded in her pursuits and behaviour. There are however works of this class in which excellent morality is joined with the most lively pictures of the human mind, and with all that can entertain the

---

[18] The *Spectator* was a magazine published by Richard Steele and Joseph Addison from 1711 to 1712 and by Addison alone in 1714; the *Guardian* was published by Richard Steele in 1713. The *Rambler* was published by John Payne from 1750 to 1752 and contained moral essays, most of them written by Dr Samuel Johnson. It inspired the *Adventurer*, produced by John Hawkesworth from 1752 to 1754. These periodicals were later re-issued as collected volumes.

imagination and interest the heart. But I must repeatedly exhort you never to read anything of the sentimental kind without taking the judgment of your best friends in the choice; for I am persuaded that the indiscriminate reading of such kind of books corrupts more female hearts than any other cause whatsoever.

— 4 —
Stéphanie de Genlis

The life of Stéphanie-Félicité Ducrest du Saint Aubin, Comtesse de Genlis (1746–1830), was as dramatic as one of her many novels. In her youth she was the mistress of a duke, but in later life she made a show of strict religious piety. Both her husband and her lover were guillotined, but she survived to see one of her pupils become the last king of France. She lived to the age of eighty-four and published over 140 works, one of which was for thirty years the most popular book on education in Europe. She defined herself as a writer, an educator and a moralist; she was also a furious polemicist and a violent opponent of contemporary French philosophy, including the works of Rousseau.

Stéphanie was born into the provincial French nobility, and claimed to have received no early education other than what she could glean from the family's servants. It was not until the age of seven that she gained access to her father's library, but she did learn to play the harp and displayed real talent on the instrument. This proved useful when the family suffered a financial crisis: her father died when she was seventeen, his health broken by a spell in a debtors' prison, and Stéphanie's mother was reduced to raising money by putting on concerts in Parisian salons to display her daughter's skill.

In the course of one of his attempts to save the family fortunes, Stéphanie's father had sailed to San Domingo, where he was captured by the English and briefly imprisoned. A fellow captive was the young, dashing nobleman Charles-Alexis, Count of Genlis, whom he regaled with stories of his beautiful daughter. When the Count returned to Paris he sought her out: the two immediately fell in love and married secretly, to the outrage of his family. By the age of twenty-one she had given birth to two daughters, and a son who was to die of measles at the age of five.

Stéphanie's aunt now introduced her into Parisian society, with its glittering round of balls, theatres and salons. Around this time she met Rousseau, who dined several times with her and her husband before he turned against them, as he did with many of his friends and supporters. Stéphanie had at this point not read any of his works, and hearing of his unconventional views on religion, she declined to do so for ten years. Towards the end of her life she produced a censored version of *Émile*, deleting all the comments she considered to be contrary to religion and morality.

In 1772, when Stéphanie was twenty-five, she became lady-in-waiting to the Duchess of Chartres. This was a remarkable social elevation, for the Orléans family would succeed to the throne should their Bourbon relatives die without issue; the two branches of the royal family already regarded each other with grave suspicion. Within days of her arrival, the Duke of Chartres had taken her as his mistress; their liaison lasted seven years and was tolerated by Stéphanie's husband, though the Duchess was blissfully unaware of it and remained her devoted friend. Stéphanie organised a course of studies for herself and the young Duchess, with tutors in geography, natural history and painting. She herself learned English and Italian, physics, and chemistry, and avidly read books from the royal library.

In 1779 Stéphanie became governess to the Duke's twin daughters, and moved to the Château de Bellechasse with the princesses, her own two daughters and her mother. Soon afterwards two young English girls joined the group, supposedly to enable the princesses to practise their English; the air of mystery surrounding them convinced most observers that they were in fact the natural daughters of Stéphanie and the Duke of Chartres. They were the first of nineteen children she was to adopt during the course of her long life.

Madame de Genlis had discovered her vocation: to be an 'educator' of children. Her move to Bellechasse coincided with the publication of her first work: a selection of children's plays printed as *Theatre for the Use of Young People*.[1] The subscription list was headed by the king and queen and was filled in five days; the book was acclaimed by critics and hugely popular with the public. It appeared two years later in English, and she presented a copy to Queen Charlotte, wife of George III. Catherine the Great had it translated into Russian, and it also found a place in the library of Catherine's daughter-in-law, the Czarina Marina Feodorovna.

In January 1782 the Duke of Chartres shocked society by putting Madame de Genlis in charge of the education of his sons as well as his daughters, a move that would have been regarded as eccentric in any family, but in the case of three young princes was positively scandalous, since it meant that the training of three boys who were in line to the throne was consigned to their father's thirty-six-year-old mistress. The male tutors resigned in disgust, but the Duke continued to support her, and she found herself in a position of unique command over her pupils.

The same month saw the publication of what would prove to be one of Madame de Genlis's most famous and influential works. Entitled *Adèle et Théodore* and subtitled *Letters on Education*,[2] this took the form of an epistolary novel, but was also a treatise setting out her views on the best way

---

[1] *Théâtre à l'Usage de la Jeunesse*, 7 vols (Paris: Lambert & Baudouin, 1779).
[2] *Adèle et Théodore, ou Lettres sur l'Éducation*, 3 vols (Paris: Lambert & Baudoin, 1782).

of educating children, and particularly girls. She later stated that she wrote the book largely as a response to the principles of female education set out in *Émile*. It was a publishing phenomenon, running into twenty-nine editions over the following thirty years, and was translated into English, Spanish, Italian, Dutch, Polish and Russian. The *English Review* described *Adèle et Théodore* as 'by much the best system of education ever published in France', an implicit disapproval of Rousseau's *Émile*, which was widely known in England.[3] A new translation was published in 1784 and it was serialised several times in British magazines during the 1780s. Genlis made two extended visits to England, in 1785 and 1788, and was fêted as a celebrated author, granted an audience with the queen and applauded in literary circles. Her book was read with approval by Jane Austen (who mentioned it in *Emma*), Fanny Burney, Catharine Macaulay, Mary Wollstonecraft and Hannah More. Maria Edgeworth even attempted her own translation.

But the adventures that Genlis's pupils were about to experience were far more dramatic than anything derived from their governess's imagination. When the Estates-General assembled at Versailles in June in response to a national financial crisis, its delegates included both her husband and her former lover, who had become Duke of Orléans. Madame de Genlis encouraged Louis-Philippe, the Duke's eldest son, to attend meetings of the Jacobin Club and took her pupils to witness the demolition of the Bastille. The supporters of the king strongly suspected that she was part of a conspiracy to put Orléans on the throne in his cousin's place.

When the Duke voted in favour of the king's execution and his earlier relationship with Genlis became a matter of public knowledge, her friends in England closed their doors to her. In 1793 the Jacobins took control of the National Assembly and both her husband and the Duke went to the guillotine. Genlis went into exile, first in Switzerland and then in Germany, where she supported herself by publishing books in a wide range of genres: historical novels, moral fables in verse, a handbook on baby care and a collection of prayers for children. Desperate for money, she also gave private lessons in French and music.

She returned to Paris in 1800 and made an accommodation with Napoleon, who gave her a pension. She continued to write (twenty-six volumes between 1806 and 1814), including a handbook of court etiquette, an eight-volume self-justifying memoir, and a series of historical novels based on the lives of famous women of the seventeenth century. The message of these books (and Madame de Genlis always had a message) was that the reign of Louis XIV was the golden age of French literature and society: language was then at its most pure and refined, society was polite and elegant, and religion was respected. The

---

[3] *English Review*, August 1783, pp. 106–09.

following century, by contrast, was a period of decline, driven by the impious and uncouth writing of the *philosophes*, and culminating inexorably in the disastrous excesses of the Revolution.

Undeterred by the sarcasm of her critics, she became a celebrity; Maria Edgeworth and her father were among her many visitors. She wrote vast numbers of letters, continued to play the harp, and even for a short time published a newspaper, in which most of the articles were written by herself. Everywhere she went, she adopted children and educated them in her own manner. She died in 1830, six months after her former pupil Louis-Philippe ascended to the throne of France.

Adèle et Théodore was always her most famous and influential work, enjoyed perhaps not so much for its didactic passages as for three lengthy gothic tales, whose plots include a girl forced by her harsh father to become a nun and a young wife locked in a dungeon by her cruel husband, their complications invariably caused by the unreasonable behaviour of men and the failure of girls to confide in their mothers.

The main character in the novel is the Baroness d'Almane (a cypher for Genlis herself), who has decided in true Rousseau style that in order to give her children a proper moral upbringing, she must take them away from the distractions and corruptions of Paris and retire to her country estate, where they will be constantly under their mother's watchful eye. Though the children are given long reading lists, it is clear that, where their moral formation is concerned, Genlis believed in learning through doing: for example, when Adèle eats too many cakes at a party, her mother lets her make herself ill before pointing out that she has brought the problem upon herself. But this is far from Rousseau's 'negative education', where children are shielded from serious harm but otherwise allowed to work things out for themselves; in fact they are barely for a moment left to their own devices. The Baroness constantly creates little dramas which will force her daughter to make a choice of actions, carefully designed to teach her to be kind and considerate to those less fortunate than herself.

Genlis constantly wrote about the dangers of love and sex, and taught that only by suppressing passion can a woman avoid suffering. Adèle learns that 'rational people, though possessed of great sensibility, will never be violently in love'. Those women in the book who give way to dissipation are invariably destined to lose their reputation, their money, their friends and their looks. The moral of the story is that the best solution for women is complete submission to the will of God and the conventions of society, and the consolation of a clear conscience.

Madame d'Almane devotes ten years of unceasing care to her children's education, but it is made clear that, despite Adèle's extensive reading list and attendance at lectures on philosophy, chemistry and natural history, there is no intention that she should become learned. As her mother explains:

> I only mean to give her a little knowledge of these things which may serve to amuse her sometimes, and prevent her from being tired at any time, should her father, her brother or her husband choose to talk on such subjects; at the same time it will preserve her from an infinite number of prejudices which are adopted by ignorance.[4]

This may appear a shockingly unambitious objective for such a lengthy pedagogical programme, but like a number of other women in this collection, Genlis preached that a retired domestic existence is the best way for a woman to achieve happiness, whilst claiming for herself the right to publish, argue and be taken seriously in the public sphere. She justified this apparent contradiction by claiming that an exception should be made for 'women of genius', whose outstanding talents gave them the right to step outside the normal restrictions imposed on women, and also by insisting that she should not be criticised because her works, unlike those of the *philosophes*, were always moral and virtuous.

Genlis later became more outspoken about the unfairness of the restrictions put around women of talent. In *Tales of the Castle*, which she published in 1785 and which outsold even *Adèle et Theodore*,[5] she inserted a section on female artists, protesting against the way they were ignored and deprecated by male critics; a girl of talent would be told she was incapable of painting historical scenes and should stick to flowers: 'thus is she discouraged, and thus is the fire of her ambition stifled; she paints roses; she was born, perhaps, to paint heroes'. Men make similar efforts to put constraints around women with literary ability:

> A man of letters, whose daughter gives evidence of wit, and a love of poetry, may be induced to cultivate these talents; but what will his first care be? Why, to rob the young scholar of that confidence which inspires fortitude, and that ambition which surmounts difficulties. He prescribes bounds to her efforts and commands her not to go beyond them [...] so the teacher traces a narrow circle round his young pupil over which she is forbid to step. Has she the genius of Corneille or Racine, she is constantly told to write nothing but novels, pastorals or sonnets [...] Had all the other arts, as well as this, been less the fruit of education and study than the happy gifts of nature, there is no doubt but there would have existed a perfect equality between men and women.[6]

---

[4] *Adelaïde and Theodore*, ed. by Gillian Dow (London: Pickering & Chatto, 2007), p. 397.
[5] *Les Veillées du Château* was first published in 1782: between that date and 1874 there were at least sixty printings in France, Britain, America, Germany, Spain, Italy and Belgium. See Anne L Schroder, 'Going Public against the Academy in 1784: Mme de Genlis Speaks out on Gender Bias', *Eighteenth-Century Studies*, 32, 3 (1999), 376–82.
[6] *Tales of the Castle: or, Stories of Instruction and Delight*, trans. by Thomas Holcroft, 5 vols (London: G. Robinson, 1785), IV, pp. 67–68.

In the preface to a later work entitled *The Influence of Women on French Literature* she again blamed women's inadequate education for their failure to produce works of great literature:

> Literary men have an advantage over female authors for a reason that is certainly impossible to misunderstand or to dispute: that all the works by women put together are not equal to a few fine pages from Bossuet[7] and Pascal[8] and a few scenes from Corneille, Racine, Molière,[9] etc.; but we should not conclude that women are constitutionally inferior to men. Genius is made up of all the qualities that they indisputably possess and that they may possess to the highest degree: imagination, sensibility, exaltation of soul. Lack of study and education has through the ages kept women away from a literary career, so they have shown their greatness of soul not by rehashing historical facts or presenting ingenious fictions in writing, but through their own actions.[10]

Madame de Genlis was very familiar with Rousseau's *Émile*, and adopted many of his precepts on child-centred education. However, she did not approve of his views on women, and made a perceptive observation on his dangerously seductive literary charms:

> It is to women that *Émile* owes its greatest success: all women in general praise Rousseau with enthusiasm, despite the fact that no author has ever treated them with less consideration. He categorically denied that they can display genius or even superior talent; he accused them all without exception of artifice and coquetry; in short, he loved them but did not respect them. He acknowledged their charms better than anyone; he spoke of them with contempt but with the voice of passion, and passion was enough to excuse everything.[11]

In the preface and notes to the second edition of *Adèle et Théodore*, Genlis was even more damning of Rousseau, accusing him of plagiarism[12] and claiming that while his 'zealous partisans' had accused her of not giving sufficient praise to *Émile*, she feared she had not been sufficiently critical of a book that was reprehensible in so many ways. She also pointed out Rousseau's hypocrisy in denouncing parents who did not raise their own children, while sending his own five infants to the foundling hospital.

---

[7] Jacques-Bénigne Bossuet (see note 16 to the previous excerpt) was considered a great orator and master of style, as expressed in his many sermons, funeral orations and theological works.
[8] Blaise Pascal (1623–1662) experienced a religious conversion in 1654, and favoured the Jansenist sect. His writing style was much admired.
[9] These three were the greatest French dramatists of the seventeenth century.
[10] *De l'Influence des Femmes sur la Littérature Française* (Paris: Maradan, 1811), p. iii.
[11] Adèle et Théodore, I, p. 169.
[12] Among the authors she claimed he had plagiarised were John Locke and François Fénelon.

Genlis, on the other hand, had practical experience of educating young children, and appears to have been very good at it. Her school at Bellechasse included her nephew César and orphan niece as well as the four Orléans children, her own daughters and the two English girls. For eight months of the year they moved from Paris to the countryside, and benefited from long walks and open-air exercise. Her pupils followed a strict timetable, with regular hours and a simple diet. These children who would otherwise, typically for their class, have been neglected by their parents and indulged by their servants, benefited from the firm but benevolent discipline of a mother-figure who showed them affection but also had high expectations of their conduct. The Baroness d'Almane was without doubt the *alter ego* of the Countess of Genlis.

Note on the Text

The 1783 English translation was based on the French first edition, published in Paris in 1782 by Lambert & Baudouin. In 1784 Genlis published a second edition with the addition of a preface and notes, and the English translation was promptly updated. The unnamed translators described themselves as 'some Ladies, who through misfortunes, too common at this time, are reduced from ease and opulence, to the necessity of applying, to the support of life, those accomplishments which were given them in their youth, for the amusement and embellishment of it'.

❖

Stéphanie-Félicité Ducrest de Saint Aubin, Countess de Genlis
Adelaide and Theodore, or Letters on Education
London: C. Bathurst & T. Cadell, 1783

Volume I, Letter IX. From the Baroness d'Almane to the Viscountess de Limours

The education of men and women agree in this particular, that it is essential to both that their vanity should be placed on things of consequence, but it differs in almost every other respect.[13] We must be careful not to inflame the minds of women, or raise them above themselves. They are born for a domestic and dependent situation, and ought to possess mildness, sensibility, and a just way of reasoning. They should have resources against idleness, with great moderation in their inclinations, and no passions. Genius is for them a useless and a dangerous gift; it lifts them out of their proper sphere, or serves

---

[13] In fact the education of Adèle and Théodore as described in the book differs very little.

to disgust them with it. Love leads them astray. Ambition teaches them to intrigue; a taste for learning makes them appear singular, and deprives them of the domestic simplicity and tenderness, and of that society of which they are so great an ornament. Formed for the management of household matters, and for the education of their children, dependant on a husband, who by turns requires their submission and their council [sic], it is necessary they should have method, prudence, patience, and a just way of thinking, that they may be able to converse with propriety on all subjects, and possess all those talents which render them pleasing; that they may have a taste for reading and reflection, without displaying their knowledge, and that they may feel the passion of love without giving themselves up to enthusiasm. [...]

Volume I, Letter x. From the Viscountess de Limours to the Baroness d'Almane

I have some doubts to propose to you on that part of your letter concerning women. It appears to me that you require a union of amiable qualities and talents, which can only fall to the lot of a very small number. You would have a woman possess solid reasoning, with all the important virtues; a knowledge of all the modern languages, without pedantry or affectation; and that, in short, she should conduct her domestic affairs like a good housewife, who pretends to no other merit. I see plainly, if your pupil is born with a superior understanding, you may make her truly accomplished: but do you expect it, if she has only a common one, and an indifferent memory? It appears to me that a plan of education ought neither to be made for prodigies or monsters. Stupidity and depravity are as rare as heroism and genius. But it is for persons of moderate talents we ought to labour, as from them we may expect most success. With regard to talents, is it not necessary the inclination should assist your cares? I had all kinds of masters. I learned Geography, Arithmetic, History, and Music. Ten years I played on the harpsichord, and learned to draw, but yet I understood nothing of all this. For dancing I had a real taste, and six months instruction made me one of the best dancers in the school. Besides, I can scarcely believe that the length of time one is obliged to give to these kind of studies, is not extremely hurtful to the production and growth of more essential qualities. I know you may be quoted as an exception to this rule; but I only speak in general. You want to cultivate the understanding, and form the mind of your daughter. How can you do this, if she learns to embroider, to draw, to dance, to sing, and to play on several instruments? In short, you propose teaching her so many things, that I am in pain for her health, and I cannot persuade myself, but that such application must be dangerous to a child. [...]

Volume 1, Letter XI. From the Baroness d'Almane to the Viscountess de Limours

And now, my dear friend, I am going to endeavour to answer your objections on the principles of education. You cannot conceive how I shall be able to improve the understanding of my pupils, and to form her heart, and at the same time to give her every agreeable qualification. In effect, if you suppose I have any hopes of seeing Adelaide, at twelve years old, an excellent musician, playing on several instruments, understanding History, Geography, Mythology, and accounts, with many of our best Works, &c. &c. your reflections would then have been perfectly just. But if such had been my plan, I needed only to have adopted the method commonly followed. But the little success obtained by these, has well justified the necessity of taking others. Rousseau observes, that the principal fault of every Tutor is from endeavouring to make his pupils shine, more than to convince their reason. With this intention, he gives them lessons which are above their comprehensions, and so load the memory, not with useful things, but with words that have in general no sense in them. Adelaide, at twelve years old, far from being a prodigy, will perhaps appear to some people infinitely less instructed than many other children of her age. She will not know a word of all those books which young people learn by heart. She will never have read Fontaine's Fables, Telemachus, Madame de Sevigny's Letters, the Works of Corneille, Racine, Crebillon, and Voltaire, &c.[14] Is it not absurd to put all these books into the hands of a child, who can comprehend nothing of them, and by that means deprive her of the pleasure of reading them when her judgment is riper? Adelaide, at twelve years old, will neither be capable of making any extracts, or of writing good letters, or of assisting in doing the honours of my house. She will have but few ideas, but they will be rational ones. She will read music well, and play on several instruments. She will draw in a surprizing manner for her age, without her master's retouching any of her performances; and by that means teaching her to tell a falsehood, instead of improving her in the art of drawing. She will neither understand history, mythology, nor geography, except what she has gained in our tapestry conversation, and other methods, which I shall mention hereafter. In this respect I think she will be better instructed than children in general. She will have many other accomplishments, which will only be discovered by living with her, and which

---

[14] Most of these were the leading French writers of the seventeenth century. The *Fables* of Jean de la Fontaine (1621-1695) were moral poems popular with children. Archbishop François Fénelon (1651-1715) wrote *Télémaque*, an epic poem designed to teach his pupil, the Duc de Bourgogne, about the dangers of absolute monarchy. The *Letters* of the Marquise de Sévigné (1626-1696) to her daughter were published from 1734 and were popular throughout Europe. Pierre Corneille (1606-1684) and Jean Racine (1639-1699) were the leading writers of tragedies for the French stage. Prosper Jolyot de Crébillon (1674-1762) was a playwright. Voltaire (1694-1778) was the only writer still living.

she has acquired in the form of amusements. [...]

Volume III, Letter XXVIII. *From the Baroness d'Almane to Madame de Valmont*

My children are not yet in the world;[15] but, as we sup at half past nine, Theodore sups with us, but goes to bed before eleven, and his father retires with him. I remain with my company until near one. Adelaide sups in her own room with Miss Bridget and the little Hermine[16] at eight; therefore she always gets up two or three hours before me. Although in that time Miss Bridget presides over her studies, I take care to direct them in such a manner that I may judge at my waking, how well she has employed her time. For example, I do not allow her to practise music; but I make her draw, write, and cast accounts. She is at present taking Extracts from history, in English and Italian, which will accustom her to write those languages, without being obliged to dedicate a particular hour to that study. She takes extracts in French from the Plays and Letters which I have written. When I am up, I correct the faults in her style and language. Afterwards I make her sing, and play on the harp[17] till noon, when, if the weather permits, she walks or reads. We all dine together at one; after dinner she embroiders, or works tapestry for half an hour. From three to five she is engaged with her two masters for singing and dancing. We then are shut up in my closet, and read an hour. At six the academy begins. She draws by the lamp and from nature.

You see, Madame, from this relation, that Adelaide is engaged in a new study. She begins to paint miniatures: she will keep this Master till she is eighteen, and during that time she will spend two hours every day in drawing. Being accustomed by degrees to be always employed, and never to lose a moment, this continued application cannot fatigue her; the variety of her occupations will refresh her. Moreover, having surmounted all the first difficulties, study will in general appear much more agreeable than painful to her, and a habit of labour will make idleness insupportable.

I procure her three times a week a recreation equally amusing and instructive. Directly after dinner I get into my carriage with my two children, and we visit the cabinets of pictures, gems, medals, or we see fine monuments or manufactories: if it is manufactories, we never fail, before we set out, to read in the Encyclopaedia[18] an explanation of what we are going to see, by which

---

[15] Adèle is now fifteen, and many children would at this age have been introduced into the 'world', in other words to Parisian society. The Baroness clearly entertained her own circle of friends, which her husband was not expected to join.
[16] Miss Bridget was the English governess, and Hermine an orphan girl adopted by Adèle.
[17] Most girls were taught the piano, but Madame de Genlis was herself an excellent harpist and had a preference for the instrument.
[18] The *Encyclopédie, ou dictionnaire raisonné des sciences, des arts et des métiers* was

means we perfectly comprehend all that is done; and we shall continue this kind of course till May.

published between 1751 and 1772. Its editors were Denis Diderot and Jean Le Rond d'Alembert, both of them *philosophes* whose anti-clerical and anti-monarchist ideas were despised by Genlis, and some of its articles were overtly political. It is noticeable that Mme d'Almane controls the children's access to this book.

— 5 —
John Bennett

The Rev. John Bennett was an obscure provincial clergyman. Little is known about his life, save that he was the curate of St Mary's Church, Manchester. He once spent five weeks in Bath, but does not appear to have travelled abroad, and his writings on women's education were not based on direct experience, since he admitted that he had no daughter of his own. This did not prevent him from expressing decisive opinions on the subject.

Bennett was a conservative man, on the Evangelical wing of the Church of England, and was opposed to freethinking and radical notions. His *Strictures on Female Education; chiefly as it Relates to the Culture of the Heart* was only a moderate success in Britain, with two Dublin editions following its first London edition in 1787.[1] It did, however, gain a considerable following in the United States, with four editions appearing between 1791 and 1798, in Philadelphia, Hartford and Worcester. John Adams gave his wife Abigail a copy of the book, and she wrote to him in January 1795 to say that Bennett was one of her favourite authors, for two reasons: 'The first is, that he is ingenious enough to acknowledge and point out the more than Egyptian bondage to which the female sex have been subjugated from the earliest ages;[2] and in the second place, that he has added his mite to the cultivation and improvement of the female mind'.[3]

Strictures has the style of an extended sermon, setting out to demolish arguments and reprove behaviour. Bennett followed it up in 1789 with another book devoted to women, *Letters to a Young Lady on a Variety of Useful and Interesting Subjects, calculated to Improve the Heart, to Form the Manners and Enlighten the Understanding*. This was a conduct book in epistolary form, giving advice to a young girl who has lost her father, and was highly derivative of previous works, as the critic in the *Monthly Review* complained, saying that its observations and reflections 'are such that, had we not already met

---

[1] John Bennett, *Strictures on Female Education; chiefly as it relates to the culture of the heart* (London: T. Cadell, J. J. & G. Robinson, J. Rivington, 1787).
[2] According to the Old Testament, the children of Israel when exiled to Egypt were kept in a state of abject slavery. Abigail Adams clearly felt this was analogous to the history of women.
[3] Woody Holton, *Abigail Adams* (New York: Atria, 2009), p. 292.

with others of exactly the same import in the volumes of Dr Fordyce and Mrs Chapone, we might bestow on them the highest praise'.[4]

Despite this cool critical reception, *Letters to a Young Lady* was to have an astonishing and long-lived success. It had three London editions, in 1789, 1795 and 1803, and was also published in Dublin. But once more it was in the United States that the book became a bestseller. There were five editions in the 1790s, including the major publishing centres of Hartford, Philadelphia and Boston, but even more remarkably it continued to be printed well into the following century, with seven more editions, the final one as late as 1856.

The first sentence of *Strictures* suggests that we may be about to read a proto-feminist work, since it refers to 'the natural equality of women with the other sex'. However, it soon becomes clear that Bennett is referring to moral rather than social equality, and he is as adamant as Rousseau in his belief that women's place in society is entirely domestic, and their virtues are different from — indeed opposite to — those of men. Their education must be designed to prepare them for their role in life, as pleasant companions to their husbands and devoted mothers of their children.

Bennett nevertheless expresses sympathy with women, since men place high expectations on them but then fail to design a system of education that would enable them to achieve these goals, and when they inevitably fall short, 'we fail not to load them with the heaviest censure, ridicule and contempt'. He admits that women have been condemned and vilified by men from the foundation of the world, and in his first chapter gives an extended history, starting from the garden of Eden and proceeding through the Egyptians, Babylonians, Assyrians, Greeks and Romans, to demonstrate how badly they all treated women. During these periods, women were treated cruelly by men, as slaves and inferior beings. (This was no doubt the section that appealed to Abigail Adams.)[5]

Paradoxically, Bennett then claims that the women of ancient Egypt were admitted to public lectures in philosophy and, in a way unparalleled and unheard of in any other country, entrusted with political negotiations, commercial interests, and other public undertakings; this was 'attempting to make them move in a sphere for which Nature never gave them talents, nor providence designed them'.

During the so-called Age of Chivalry, women were not oppressed but honoured by men, but Bennett regards this approach as equally misguided. He cannot believe that the adulation men expressed for women at that time was

---

[4] *Monthly Review*, Art. III (Jan–April 1790), I, p. 255.
[5] Long passages in this chapter appear to have been derived from *Essai sur le Caractère, les Mœurs et l'Esprit des Femmes dans les Différens Siècles*, a work published in 1772 by the Frenchman Antoine-Léonard Thomas (Paris: Moutard, 1772). It had been translated into English by a Mr Russell (London: G. Robinson, 1773) and by Jemima Kindersley (London: J. Dodsley, 1781). The latter version is referenced by Bennett.

sincere, and assumes it was an affectation or a form of flattery. The Renaissance period had the unfortunate effect of putting certain women in a position to become men's intellectual rivals: they were taught the learned languages of Latin and Greek, studied philosophy and theology, and published their own opinions. This was to fall into the opposite error, since it diverted women from their true function:

> And though when this rage expired, their abilities were carried to an extraordinary height under the powerful workings of an unnatural enthusiasm, they were but disgusting monuments of talents misapplied, and of taste misdirected. A woman issuing out laws, disputing in philosophy, haranguing the Pope in Latin, writing Greek, studying Hebrew, commencing theologian and preaching in public, may be a literary heroine that challenges our wonder, but has nothing of that softness, timidity and reserve which in that sex so powerfully captivate our hearts and enchant our imaginations.[6]

Bennett then turns from history to geography, condemning the continuing oppression of women around the world. There was, however, one country that was exempt from these faults: 'the condition of women in England no doubt may be justly pronounced to be supremely happy', for 'if Europe has been called the Paradise of the sex, Britain seems to be the choicest spot of this Paradise, in which the sovereign Former has deigned to place the fairest of the fair, and munificently to distil upon their favoured heads the richest of his sweets'.

Bennett is compelled to admit that there are respected women writers in England, and politely praises Hester Chapone, as well as the historian Catharine Macaulay Graham, the classicist Elizabeth Carter and the poet Anna Seward. He also describes the work of Madame de Genlis as 'a treasure to young ladies'. But he falls back on the usual excuse that these women are exceptions to the rule and therefore do not invalidate his argument. Worse than this, they represent a sort of monstrous aberration: 'There are uncommon meteors in the planetary world. There are eccentric bodies in the heavens, which challenge our amazement. There are females enriched with an etherial spirit which mounts up to its kindred skies [...] But prodigies of female genius do not prove at all the general state of female talents, or the ordinary level of female understanding'. Bennett's educated women will occupy a happy medium between two extremes; his system will be one 'which shall administer a proper share of principles and taste and, whilst it does not exalt a woman to an unnatural and invidious eminence, does not depress her to an abject state of frivolousness, insipidity and contempt'.

From what Bennett has heard of the situation in France, women there have moved far beyond their sphere by daring to be not only writers themselves

---

[6] John Bennett, *Strictures* (Dublin: Pat Wogan, 1798), pp. 33–34.

but also critics of men's writing. He regards this as positively diseased: female literature 'is swelled beyond its natural dimensions. To sit as judges upon literary productions is intruding on the prerogative of the other sex. I want not a plethora, but a sound and undistended state of the female understanding.'

The second chapter describes itself as a 'philosophical theory of the progress of love', and surveys the development of relations between the sexes, from primitive societies where women were treated with cruelty to the modern day, when society has become 'effeminate': instead of living in proper domestic retirement, women are seen too much in public, where men flatter, or worse still, seduce them. Although in his later *Letters to a Young Lady*, Bennett criticised Rousseau's *Émile*, saying that 'Nothing was ever so strangely romantic as his Emilius, or system of Education; a mere paper edifice of children, which the first and gentlest touch of experience totally destroys', in *Strictures* his sentimental image of a mother surrounded by her children is almost identical to that described by Rousseau. Indeed, his condemnation of English women as infected by French influence, wasting their time in foolish diversions and indulging in indiscretion, intrigue and infidelity, is as violent as Rousseau's, and his insistence that they should adopt maternity as their sole important aim in life is precisely in line with Rousseau's philosophy. Women are at present the 'bane and corrupters of society', bearing the responsibility for male dissipation, and it will take no less than a revolution to return them to the home where they belong.

In a chapter on the talents of women, Bennett entered into a discussion that had been continuing for over a century. It was generally accepted that women thought in a different way from men, but it was a matter of some controversy as to whether this was because their brains were physically different, or their many domestic duties did not leave them time to study, or as some women would complain, men deliberately kept them in a state of ignorance in order better to subjugate them.

It was widely believed that women compensated for their intellectual deficiency through increased 'sensibility' or feeling. Their exquisite sensitivity made them aware through intuition of things that men, with their more logical reasoning, might not appreciate. This sensibility gave women an active imagination, but their thinking was superficial: they were not able to 'combine' ideas in the way Locke had described, and since all their thoughts derived from physical sensations, they were incapable of abstract reasoning. They were, however, superior in matters of taste, which required natural talent rather than profound thought.

These theories were willingly accepted by Bennett, since they were consistent with his views on the different social roles of men and women. God in his providence had designed men to be active in public affairs and women to live a life of domestic retirement, and had given them the physical and mental characteristics that would enable them to fulfil these functions appropriately.

Bennett admits that culture has an important impact on the development of men and women, but is still convinced that there is a real underlying difference in their intellects. His key argument is that men and women have been designed 'providentially', that is, by the deliberate intention of God, to be counterparts of one another. Here he is entirely aligned with Rousseau (who preferred to talk of Nature rather than God), and with his view that education should be designed to strengthen these natural predilections, and that any attempt by either sex to be more like the other is a monstrous aberration.

His reference to 'the sentence of subordination' in Genesis puts Bennett into an older tradition of overtly anti-women works, going back centuries, that sought to bring any dispute over the relative merits of the sexes to an end by claiming divine authority. He ceases trying to persuade his audience and instead proclaims with the authority of the pulpit that women 'were not formed for political eminence or literary refinement', and that if they were encouraged to become writers, not only would the order of nature be reversed but the human population would be much reduced, since all such women would be unmarriageable and compelled to remain virgins. With this fine if rather absurd peroration, Bennett concludes his essay on the talents of women.

❖

John Bennett
Strictures on Female Education; Chiefly as it Relates to the Culture of the Heart
Dublin: Pat Wogan, 1798 (3rd edn)

Chapter 2: Observations on the manner in which the treatment of the sex will be influenced by, and will reciprocally influence the taste, the sentiments, the habits and pursuits, the manners, the morals, the public and the private happiness of a people.

Why indeed had woman her existence, but to dignify and ennoble it by such superior employments? When does she appear to so much advantage, as when, surrounded in her nursery by a train of prattlers, she is holding forth the moral page for the instruction of one, and pouring out the milk of health to invigorate the frame and constitution of another? When is her snowy bosom half so serene, or when thrills it with such an innocent and pleasing rapture, as in these silent moments of domestic attention, or these attitudes of undissembled love? What painter, wandering with a creative fancy over all the exhaustless riches of nature, can give us so enchanting and delightful a picture in so elegant a frame?

What pleasures of the *Levee*, the Drawing Room, or *Masquerade*[7] can vie, in flavour, with these more retired, maternal satisfactions? And when can woman ever be said to consult the real dignity and happiness of her sex, but when she is thus conscientiously discharging her duty to the man to whom she has plighted, at the altar of her God, her vows and her affections?

Such maternal culture, such a revolution in the sentiments and conduct of that sex, would be attended with the happiest advantages. An alteration would soon be visible on the face of society. If the minds of women were placed upon solid objects, by a judicious and early culture, they would become at once the ornament and blessing, as now there is but too much reason to apprehend, that they are only the bane and corrupters of society. Their charms would be the stimulating prize of valour, merit, understanding. Their conversation would be a soft but powerful spur to every noble action; and in the intervals which would be then devoted to their company, the soul would be acquiring an elasticity and a vigour for every great and dignified undertaking.

Little do women know of their own *real* interests, if they do not think themselves essentially interested in such a revolution. They would then be approached with esteem and veneration. The frothiness of compliment would gradually be changed into the language of truth. Their empire over our hearts, then, founded on the immutable qualities of the mind, would be glorious and permanent, not subject to expire in the wrinkles of age, or wither with the transient roses of beauty. Their conversation would give cheerfulness and delicacy of sentiment; and ours would give instruction. There would be a gentle conflict and emulation of talent, and both parties would be mutually improved by the mutual collision. Their friendship would be courted, and our morals would be improved. In the refinement of our taste, we should disdain to stoop for pleasure to an harlot; we should look for real enjoyment with women who had sentiment and understanding.

Chapter 3: A disquisition concerning the nature, quality and extent of female talents, and the comparative difference of understanding in the sexes.

The nature of my undertaking calls for some reflexions on the quality, the degree and extent of female talents. And this will involve me in the hackneyed comparison which has so frequently been made betwixt the natural endowments and understanding of the different sexes — an enquiry which,

---

[7] The Levée was a ceremony that began in the reign of Louis XIV, who gave audience to his courtiers after rising from bed and while being dressed by his servants. The term was extended to apply to other royal private audiences. The Drawing Room was the term used for a formal public audience during the reign of George III; these were held at St James's Palace on Thursday afternoons and Sundays after morning service. A Masquerade was a masked ball.

though it has agitated the curious and employed the pens of so many ingenious writers, does not seem to have been pursued with that disinterestedness and candour which had so much in contemplation the discovery of truth, as the supporting of a system.

The talents of women have been degraded by some to an unreasonable ebb of feebleness and frivolity, and exalted by others to as unnatural an eminence of brilliancy and distinction. In the ages immediately succeeding those of Chivalry, it was fashionable to speak of women as of prodigies in science, and to decorate with equally lavish encomiums their understanding and their charms. Nor was this taste confined merely to individuals. Even nations have been as proud of producing a list of literary heroines, as of tracing their antiquity from the remotest ages, or their origin from kings.[8] Interest, policy or fashion have continued what enthusiasm thus began.

Authors who have wished to stand well with the sex, to lie upon the toilet,[9] to be distinguished with their favours, and to acquire the reputation of gallantry and taste, have supported the same fulsome panegyrics. A rational enquirer has only to observe that if such extraordinary women ever did exist, they were only a kind of phenomena in their horizon, and neither prove the general state of female talents, nor the general superiority of female understanding. From the foot of an Hercules, there is no deducing the usual stature and proportions of a man. The Alps would give a most improper[10] idea of the common mountains and scenery of nature.

Though I am privately convinced of the absurdity of this comparison betwixt the talents of the sexes; though I conceive it to be more a matter of curiosity than use, more calculated to amuse or display ingenuity than to serve the cause of science or of truth, yet philosophers have condescended to enter into it with so much minuteness, and to enlarge upon it with so nice a discrimination, as to have rendered it a plausible, and to the general design of this work, something of a necessary and an essential investigation. They have dissected the peculiar organisation of women to discover the most latent stamina of talents, or the physical, unhappy causes which obstructed their existence. From the size, formation, temperature and quality of their brain, Aristotle, Almaricus, Malebranche[11] and many others have reasoned to their particular degree of

---

[8] Here Bennett gives a footnote referring to a list of illustrious women included in *Defence of Women*, an essay by the Spanish monk Father Benito Feijoo (1676–1764). Benito Jerónimo Feijoo y Montenegro, *Essays or Discourses*, trans. by John Brett (London: H. Payne, C. Dilly, T. Evans, 1780).

[9] That is, to have their books seen on ladies' dressing-tables.

[10] The text says 'proper'.

[11] All these writers were mentioned by Feijoo, who poured scorn on their conclusion that men's brains were superior to women's. Aristotle examined the differences between men and women in *De Generatione Animalium*; Amalric of Bena was condemned as a heretic for claiming that the existence of females was the result of human sin; Nicolas Malebranche

capacity and understanding; but whoever has read their observations must allow that such a species of research is but laborious trifling, from which no certain inferences can be drawn, and no solid or rational improvements can be reaped.

It may be supposed with great probability and fairness that their very outward frame is marked with the physical inferiority. It appears not to be calculated for such efforts of thinking as the more abstracted sciences require, and which entail on the most robust constitution even of men, languor and disease. The delicacy of the everlasting pea,[12] which so happily unites elegance with sweetness, would be easily oppressed. The tender plant, which is refreshed with gentle gales, would be entirely overwhelmed or exterminated by a whirlwind. Providence always wise, and always benevolent, has adapted the frame and organisation to their burdens. Where robustness is denied, vigorous and athletic exercises are not expected.

Principles of analogy are favourable to my argument. Observations on the brute creation confirm it. Amongst birds, beasts, insects, animals in general, the males are observed to have greater strength, courage, vigour, enterprise; females superior beauty of plumage,[13] form, proportion, more delicacy and softness, but withal an higher degree of timidity and weakness. The great God of nature is thus uniform in all his plans and in all his operations. Superiority, for the sake of order and protection, must be lodged somewhere. And it seems providentially lodged in the males. But let us not take up with this presumptive reasoning — let us rather have recourse to experience and facts.

There are but two points of view from which we can see this subject, or pursue the comparison with fairness and precision. Culture makes so great a difference in favour of *our* sex that, to discover the precise bounties of nature to each, we must compare a boy and girl at the age of six or seven; or we must look into some savage countries where both are in their primitive state of rudeness without knowledge or instruction. At this age, in point of quickness, docility and imitation, females may be pronounced to have the advantage. But this is by no means any adequate proof of their *general* superiority. Possibly the profounder thoughtfulness of the boy may obstruct the more brilliant and showy exertions. It is not the most solid bodies that sparkle most in collision. Gold does not glitter half so much as tinsel. The louring, heavy cloud involves more moisture than is contained in the glistening dew-drops of the morning.

The conceptions of a girl, instantaneous as lightning, astonish and surprise. She interests us by the liveliness with which she enters into all our instructions.

---

discussed women's brains in *De la Recherche de la Vérité*, 2 vols (Paris: Christophe David, 1721), II, ch. 1, first published 1674–75.
[12] A perennial form of the sweet pea.
[13] This is of course inaccurate, since male birds tend to have brighter plumage than females.

Her fancy gives a pleasing hue to every image she receives, and *reflects* it with advantage; nor does human life afford a more agreeable employment, than carefully to tend the beauties of this opening flower, and show them to perfection. Pitiable is the mother who knows not that such an office has sweets beyond the gaudiness of pleasure, the incense of admiration, and the essence of perfumes.

At the same time, the very nature of these qualities precludes that superiority of strong judgment and of nice discrimination, which are the more peculiar prerogative of men. Vivacity is unfavourable to profound thinking and accurate investigation. And yet it is profound thinking and accurate investigation which carry all knowledge and all literary improvements to their zenith of perfection. Even men, who are gifted with a fine imagination and the more lively talents, are frequently observed to be proportionably defective in the substantial. Whilst they cultivate the charms of poetry or the polite arts, they have not extension, subtlety or comprehensiveness of mind enough for more severe and abstracted speculations. The union of a warm and vigorous imagination with a very sound and discriminating judgment is rare indeed. Nature has conferred so rich a fortune on few of her children. Her favours are, in general, dispensed with a nicer equality, and with a seeming parsimony to individuals that has generously had in contemplation the portioning of all. In some instances, indeed, they have been blended, and they have worked miracles. The fire of Etna has boiled up in the cold and chilling regions of the North.

Savage countries do not invalidate, but strengthen this opinion. There, in general, women appear to have the advantage over the other sex, because nature displays the lively [sic], and because the substantial endowments of the mind are not unfolded by culture, or roused by emulation.

But there seems to be an error and absurdity in making the comparison. The sexes were *providentially*[14] formed as counterparts of one another. They have each of them abilities suited to the sphere in which an all-wise providence intended them to move; but as that differs *essentially* in the two sexes, so likewise does the nature of their faculties and the texture of their understanding. Who would think of contrasting the oak with the willow, or a myrtle with the delicate and almost transparent balsam? Who would compare the abilities of an Archimedes with those of an Addison?[15] Their merits were wholly opposite in their cast; yet merits they both had, which have challenged the universal admiration of the world, and to which the very latest posterity must bear an ample tribute of applause.

Let us, however, look more nearly at the contrast. Women then have a more

---

[14] That is, by the will of God.
[15] Joseph Addison, editor of the *Spectator* from 1711 to 1714, was admired for his fine writing style and sound moral principles. Archimedes was an ancient Greek mathematician.

brilliant fancy, a quicker apprehension and a more exquisite taste. When they apply their faculties to their proper studies, how wonderfully do they charm and how poignantly do they delight! In works that require the efforts of imagination only, how animated and descriptive is a woman's pen! What pictures does she exhibit! How soft are the tints, how glowing are the colours, and how impassioned the touches of her pencil!

But whether it arises from an original defect in their frame and constitution, whether it is that an unquiet imagination and ever restless sensibility afford not opportunity or leisure enough for deep meditation, it is very certain that they cannot, like the men, arrange, combine, abstract, pursue and diversify a long train of ideas, and in everything that requires the more substantial talents, must submit to a strong and a marked inferiority. The truth is that restlessness of sensibility, and that inquietude of imagination, which debar the possibility of great attainments, were providentially designed to compose the very life and essence of their graces. They are the very medium by which they please. If they were constituted to have our firmness and our depth, they would want their native and their strongest attractions. They would cease to be women, and they would cease to charm.

It may be said that judgment is principally formed by comparison and observation,[16] and that the weakness of theirs arises from their want of opportunities to improve it, the reserve of their sex, their domestic duties and sedentary life chiefly confining them to a very narrow circle, whilst business, ambition, curiosity or pleasure lead us into the world, to see various countries, manners, customs, to hear in different coffee houses, clubs and societies the sentiments of all ranks and denominations of people, and to witness characters of every kind and magnitude, of every different shade and every opposite complexion. This is all in some measure true. Still it does not account for that original difference betwixt the intellects of man and woman which is discoverable at an early period of life, for that palpable opposition of the thoughtful to the lively, of the firm to the delicate and of the profound to the cheering, which nature seems industriously to have made characteristic of the sexes.

I would ask the warmest panegyrist of women whether he can fancy that there ever existed *one* in the world who, with the utmost stretch and cultivation of her mind, could have pursued such a train of thinking as a Locke, could have combined with a Montesquieu, arranged like an Euclid, or scrutinised the secrets of nature like a Newton.[17] It is true I have mentioned only prodigies of

---

[16] This was indeed said by John Locke, in his *Essay Concerning Human Understanding* (1689), but Locke made no distinction between men and women.

[17] These men were regarded as among the greatest philosophers of all time. Euclid was an ancient Greek mathematician. John Locke (1632–1704) wrote books on the nature of thought and political organisation. Charles-Louis de Secondat (1689–1755), Baron de Montesquieu,

men. It is true that nature, by extraordinary efforts in the production of such characters, seems to have exhausted, for a considerable time, all her riches and her powers. The question, likewise, it may be urged, will always be unfair, till women have enjoyed equal advantages, and been called forth, by similar encouragements, into literary greatness. But dropping all the subtleties of argument, and reasoning only from what appears the original stamina in the minds of both, I conceive it to be a question which every man's convictions and private observations will answer in the negative, whatever tenderness to the sex may lead him to affect, or delicacy to conceal.

But here again comes in false panegyric. Women have been described with every talent that does honour to humanity. Illustrious queens, politicians, heroines glitter in the historic page. Some women have encountered the abstruseness of mathematics.[18] Others have loved to wander in the labyrinths of metaphysics. But what progress have they made? What great feats have they achieved? Let cool experience answer the question.

If we admit that such descriptions have not been exaggerated; if we could suppose that we were not treading upon fairy ground (and yet who must not have this doubt?), have any of these female efforts pleased, or have any of these *unnatural* labours gained immortality? Either they never existed at all, or they have been raised infinitely beyond the bounds of probability and truth.

As to politics, what were they, at any of the periods when women have been celebrated for their political attainments? Were they not the petty interests of as petty a territory, whose views and wants terminated chiefly in itself, without looking to any other quarter of the globe? Did they ever require that universal penetration, that comprehensiveness of research, that stretch and vigour of thought, that wonderful combination of schemes and ideas, that retrospection and anticipation, that bringing past and present into one common point of view, which the immense, diffusive, complicated concerns of large, extended kingdoms at the present, period, and in the modern circumstances of Europe, absolutely demand? It will follow from the observations, likewise, that have been already made in this essay, that women are not calculated to preside over kingdoms. They were not formed to hold the reins of empire, to penetrate into the views and wants, or to adjust the various and complicated interests of conflicting states. The reign of queens has generally been a *burlesque*

---

was a French political philosopher best known for *De l'Esprit des Lois* (Geneva: Barrillot et fils, 1748), translated into English by Thomas Nugent as *The Spirit of Laws* (London: J. Nourse & P. Vaillant, 1750). Sir Isaac Newton (1643–1727) was admired as one of the most influential mathematicians and scientists of all time.

[18] Here Bennett inserts a footnote with a long list of literary women taken from Feijoo's work referred to above. He also references Ann Thicknesse's *Sketches of the Lives and Writings of the Ladies of France* (London: W. Brown & J. Dodsley, 1778), which was dedicated to the bluestocking Elizabeth Carter.

upon government, the tyranny of some capricious favourite whom they have espoused, and whose sentiments they have adopted, in proportion as they have admired his person or address. On him have devolved all the burdens of the state, and to him has been allotted the more enviable office of apportioning the royal smiles. He has been the *real* pilot of the vessel, whilst the woman he has governed by his policy or his attractions has sat, in ostensible majesty, at the helm. Beside [sic] the political greatness of these ladies is equivocal from the peculiar circumstances of their age. Amidst a race of pigmies, a person of ordinary stature is a giant. When times are ignorant and barbarous, common knowledge is considered as a prodigy. The rustic who can spell a newspaper is at once the scholar and the oracle of his village.[19] The star that twinkles in a dark and gloomy night is welcomed as a sun.

Nor let the sex suppose me their accuser or their foe. If I have not wholly mistaken the method, I mean to be their advocate and friend. I have left them the seeds of everything that pleases and captivates in woman. Their brows were not intended to be ploughed with wrinkles, nor their innocent gaiety damped by abstraction. They are perpetually to please, and perpetually to enliven. If we were to plan the edifice, they were to furnish the embellishments. If we were to lay out and cultivate the garden, they were beautifully to fringe its borders with flowers, and fill it with perfume. If we were destined to superintend the management of kingdoms, they were to be the fairest ornaments of those kingdoms, the embellishers of society and the sweeteners of life.

If we consult scripture, we shall discover that such was the original intention of heaven in the formation of the sexes. The sentence of subordination[20] obviously implies that man should have the pre-eminence on subjects that require extensive knowledge, courage, strength, activity, talents or laborious application. Women were not formed for political eminence or literary refinement. The softness of their nature, the delicacy of their frame, the timidity of their disposition and the modesty of their sex, absolutely disqualify them for such difficulties and exertions. Their destiny of bearing and nursing children, the necessity of superintending domestic concerns, and the peculiar diseases to which they are liable, leave them little time for such public undertakings, whilst the humble offices in which they are engaged confer a blessing and a benefit upon society that are infinitely beyond the coldness of knowledge and the apathy of speculation. The wife, the mother and the economist of a family would, unfortunately, be lost in the literary pedant, the order of nature would be totally reversed, and the population of the globe preposterously sacrificed

---

[19] Newspapers were often passed from hand to hand, and literate people would read articles aloud for the benefit of those who could not read.
[20] In the story of the Garden of Eden in Genesis 3. 16, after Adam and Eve eat the apple from the Tree of the Knowledge of Good and Evil, God punishes Eve by condemning her and all other women, saying 'thy desire shall be to thy husband, and he shall rule over thee'.

to the cold, forbidding pride of a studious virginity. The woman of the cloister would want the graces of a citizen of the world. In that ardour of understanding which rouses emulation, she would lose that soothing manner which conciliates and endears. The world would be deprived of its fairest ornaments, life of its highest zest, and man of that gentle bosom on which he can recline amidst the toils of labour, and the agonies of disappointment. [...]

Still let not these degraded fair ones despond. Let them not complain of their humiliating lot. Whilst virtue, taste, sensibility or discernment remain in the world, they will always have a high degree of influence and respect. Their rank, though subordinate, is not unimportant. The services they do society, though not trumpeted by fame, are recorded by gratitude and graven on the heart, and they share in the honour and distinctions of the men. Their influence often lends considerable aids in the formation of those characters which history distinguishes with its undying honours. Many are the heroes they have roused into glory. Innumerable are the statesmen they have raised by their secret magic into fame; and whenever they are tempted to repine at the appearance of insignificance and inferiority, it becomes them to remember that their greatest strength lies in their weakness, their commands in their tears; that their softness has frequently disarmed the rage of emperors and tyrants; that their blandishments have a soothing and persuasive energy which great and generous souls are seldom able to resist; that their charms have worked miracles in every age and nation, and brought about the most important revolutions of the world.

— 6 —
Catharine Macaulay Graham

Catharine Macaulay (1731–1791) was the daughter of John Sawbridge, a landowner in Kent. Her mother died when Catharine was two years old, her father was frequently absent and she was left with a governess from whom she received only a rudimentary education; she later claimed that it was a chance discovery of a book of history on a windowsill that triggered her thirst for knowledge.

The Sawbridge family were political radicals. Catharine and her brother John, who became a liberal Member of Parliament, were anti-monarchists who supported the widening of the voting franchise to the growing industrial centres, and reform of the boroughs whose MPs were chosen by a small group of landowners.

In this political battle, history was a weapon. Particularly relevant was the history of the previous century, which had seen the upheavals of the Civil War and execution of King Charles I, a short experiment with republican government followed by the restoration of the Stuarts, and the so-called Glorious Revolution of 1688 which had driven James II from the country and replaced him with William III, whose powers as monarch were circumscribed by parliament. To know someone's views on the rights and wrongs of these historic events would make it easy to guess where they would sit on the contemporary arguments about the balance of power between king and parliament, the issue of voting reform, and the complaints coming from the American colonies. To the Tories the Commonwealth was a disaster and the execution of the king an unspeakable crime; to the Whigs, the constitutional settlement imposed on William III was a model of perfect government.

In 1763, Catharine Macaulay stepped into this controversy with the first volume of a history of seventeenth-century England. This was in all respects an astonishing thing to do, for not only did women not write history, they were often discouraged from even reading about events which had no bearing on their domestic existence. Furthermore, Catharine wrote history as propaganda. She had strong views and was not afraid to state them, with none of the apologetic formulae women often used to excuse their invasion of masculine territory. Her views were overtly republican, and she interpreted the country's history as a struggle between an oppressive aristocratic class and a subjugated populace that went back to the invasion of England by the Normans in 1066.

At the rather advanced age of twenty-nine, Catharine had married a Scottish physician, Dr George Macaulay, and although some commentators took the predictable view that the book must have been the work of her husband, she became a widely celebrated author: Horace Walpole wrote that she was one of the sights of London that foreigners went to see.[1]

Macaulay's status as a female historian made it easy for her opponents to refuse to engage with her ideas while mocking her failure to comply with feminine stereotypes. James Boswell quoted Samuel Johnson as saying 'she is better employed at her toilet than using her pen. It is better she should be reddening her own cheeks than blackening other people's characters'.[2] Hannah More, though an early supporter of Macaulay, later showed an equal lack of solidarity, writing contemptuously after her death that she 'was not feminine either in her writing or her manners, she was only a tolerably clever man'.[3]

Dr Macaulay died in 1766, and eight years later his widow moved to Bath. She was by now a wealthy woman deriving significant income from her books, but within a few months she made a change that intrigued and amused her contemporaries, accepting an offer from the Rev. Thomas Wilson, a seventy-three-year-old widower, to move into his house. His admiration for her soon became so intense as to be embarrassing: he transferred the freehold of his house to her, left her a large legacy in his will, and went as far as to adopt her young daughter as his child. Wilson had a life-sized marble statue of Catharine Macaulay erected in the chancel of the church of St Stephen's Walbrook in London, of which he was absentee rector.

One of Bath's residents was Dr James Graham, a Scottish society doctor who attended to Catharine Macaulay's chronic ailments, and was regarded with suspicion by some as a social climber and a smooth-talking quack. He had a younger brother, William, who was in the navy and studying to become a doctor. In December 1778, Catharine Macaulay, who was forty-seven and had been widowed for twelve years, married the twenty-one-year-old William Graham. Her male critics and political opponents were beside themselves with delight, and took pleasure in presenting Catharine Macaulay's second marriage as an example of that age-old misogynist accusation: uncontrollable female lust. According to them, there could be no explanation for her action other than sexual urges which the ageing Dr Wilson could not satisfy. Not only was the disparity in ages extreme, but so was their social standing.

It was universally assumed that Catharine Macaulay's career was now over, but following her second marriage, Macaulay took up her pen again and over

---

[1] *The Letters of Horace Walpole* (London: Richard Bentley, 1844), I, p. 227.
[2] James Boswell, *Life of Johnson* (Oxford: Oxford University Press, 1980), p. 749.
[3] Letter from Hannah More to Mrs Boscawen, 1782, in *Memoirs of the Life & Correspondence of Mrs Hannah More*, ed. by William Roberts, 4 vols (London: Seeley & Burnside, 1834), I, p. 233.

the following five years completed the eight volumes of her *History of England*. She and her husband then left for a year-long visit to America, where she was welcomed with open arms. The Americans gratefully remembered her support of their early struggles against British rule, and she was the guest of a number of the leaders of the new United States; the visit was crowned by a ten-day stay at the home of George Washington in Mount Vernon. Mercy Otis Warren described Macaulay as 'a lady of most extraordinary talent, a commanding genius, and brilliance of thought',[4] and was inspired by her example to write her own history of the American War of Independence.[5]

On returning to England, Catharine and her husband retired to the country and no longer mixed in society. However, the world had not yet heard the last of her: in 1790 she was moved to write a riposte to Edmund Burke's *Reflections on the French Revolution*, expressing her view that the dramatic political upheaval in France would lead to liberty and equality, rather than the social chaos Burke predicted. She did not live to see the Jacobin Terror vindicate Burke's opinions, for she died in June 1791 after a long illness, at the age of sixty.

She left behind her final work, entitled *Letters on Education*.[6] This was the only one of her books in which she openly addressed the position of women in society. It was, however, a subject in which she clearly had a keen interest and about which she had read extensively, for it contains numerous references to earlier writers on the subject: in particular John Locke, François Fénelon, Rousseau and Madame de Genlis. The early chapters add little to these writers' prescriptions for the treatment of young children, who should be encouraged to take physical exercise and enjoy simple pleasures, put to bed early, and neither over-indulged nor treated with excessive severity. She echoes Locke rather than Rousseau in insisting that character traits are acquired rather than innate, but shares Rousseau's view that young children should be allowed to learn from impressions and experience rather than having their minds stuffed with facts.

However, Macaulay then goes on to propose a course of study that seems likely to challenge anyone but a child prodigy. Latin, geography, physics, writing, arithmetic and French 'are fully sufficient to fill up the time of childhood'; at the age of twelve they should read Plutarch's *Lives of the Greeks and Romans* in translation, the collected volumes of Addison's *Spectator* and Mentelle's *Géographie Comparée* in the original French, memorising selected passages. At fourteen they will start Latin composition and learn history from

---

[4] Bridget Hill, *The Republican Virago: The Life and Times of Catharine Macaulay, Historian* (Oxford: Clarendon Press, 1992), p. 126.
[5] Mercy Otis Warren, *History of the American Revolution* (Boston: Manning and Loring for E. Larkin, 1805).
[6] Catherine Macaulay Graham, *Letters on Education* (London: C. Dilly, 1790).

Rollin[7] in French and Livy in the original Latin. The study of Greek begins at fifteen, together with the Latin historians and Edward Gibbon's *Decline and Fall of the Roman Empire*. Sixteen is the age for Cicero, Plutarch, Epictetus and Seneca; in English Shakespeare, Milton and Pope; and in French Boileau, Corneille, Racine, Molière and Voltaire — but not Rousseau. Astronomy, science and natural history will follow, along with politics, metaphysics and finally mathematics. (Mary Wollstonecraft wrote a favourable review of the *Letters on Education*, but was nevertheless afraid that the number of books mentioned were 'more than could be digested, unless by a youth of uncommon abilities, during the period specified'.)[8]

One notable omission from this list is the Bible: the study of sacred writings is not to begin until the age of twenty-one. The reason is that Macaulay wanted the pupil to become a Christian from conviction, through reason not authority. Children need to have developed their intellect and judgment and to understand other religions in order to appreciate the nature of Christianity, so the evidence for and against it may be examined by 'an unbiased mind'. Indeed, the exercise of judgment appears to be more important than the conclusion reached; she says with a shrug that if the pupil does not become a Christian 'he will at least be an Infidel on rational principles'.

Up to this point, Macaulay uses the masculine pronoun to refer to children, so it seems she is referring to the education of boys. However, she suddenly states that everything she has said is equally relevant to girls: 'though I have been obliged (in order to avoid confusion) to speak commonly in the masculine character [...] the same rules of education in all respects are to be observed to the female as well as to the male children', and she mocks 'the absurd notion, that the education of females should be of an opposite kind to that of males'. Her sarcastic tone continues when she complains that boys are allowed to run around as they wish, but if a girl does the same, she is reproved severely for transgressing the laws of decorum. Coming from a woman who had been viciously lampooned for her own unconventional behaviour, this must have been said with feeling.

A similar emotion can be detected in her criticism of the belief in women's intellectual inferiority. In the preface to the *Letters on Education* she reproduced the comment of a critic on her earlier philosophical work, the *Treatise on the Immutability of Moral Truth*, which said the work was 'really wonderful considering her sex'; it seems the whole book is a response to this jibe. Chapter XXI is entitled 'Morals must be taught on immutable principles', and in it

---

[7] Charles Rollin (1661–1741) was a French historian who published twelve volumes of ancient history.
[8] Mary Wollstonecraft, *The Analytical Review*, November 1790, p. 243.

Macaulay expresses her conviction that there is not one truth, or one law, or one set of virtues for men, and another for women, but that 'there is but one rule of right for the conduct of all rational beings; consequently that true virtue in one sex must be equally so in the other'.

This is key to her attitude to the purpose of education, and is much more important than a list of books to read. It is a matter of principle that 'true wisdom, which is never found at variance with rectitude, is as useful to women as to men; because it is necessary to the highest degree of happiness, which can never exist with ignorance'. As she explains to Hortensia, her fictional correspondent, what women learn is less important than the fact they become accustomed to exercising their minds. If women cannot be happy without being wise, it is immoral to keep them in ignorance. She rejects the theory that women are innately different from men and should not be educated in the same way, since their traditional faults 'do not in any manner proceed from sexual causes, but are entirely the effects of situation and education'.

Her argument is made even more explicit in the following chapter, entitled 'No Characteristic Difference in Sex'. Rousseau was of course the most famous contemporary proponent of innate sexual differences, and Macaulay attacks him with asperity. She believes that morality is the same for every human being, and ridicules his idea that the complementary virtues of man and woman can combine to create one harmonious whole. It is offensive to tell an intelligent woman that she thinks like a man. (Ironically Mary Wollstonecraft, in her review of the *Letters*, referred to Macaulay as 'this masculine and fervid writer', though she later disavowed the phrase.)

Macaulay freely admitted the faults of women in her society, but insisted that these arose not from their nature but from inadequate education, and far from sharing Rousseau's view that men and women should be educated in entirely different ways, she declared that until people gave up 'the absurd notion of sexual excellence' — the idea that the sexes had different virtues — it would be impossible to design a system of education that was good for either men or women.

❖

Catharine Macaulay Graham
Letters on Education
London: C. Dilly, 1790

Letter IV. Amusement and Instruction of Boys and Girls to be the Same

The moderns, in the education of their children, have too much followed the stiff and prudish manners of ancient days, in the separating the male and female children of a family. This is well adapted to the absurd unsocial rigour of Grecian manners; but as it is not so agreeable to that mixture of the sexes in a more advanced age which prevails in all European societies, it is not easy to be accounted for, but from the absurd notion that the education of females should be of the opposite kind to that of males. How many nervous diseases have been contracted? How much feebleness of constitution has been acquired, by forming a false idea of female excellence, and endeavouring by our art to bring Nature to the ply of our imagination? Our sons are suffered to enjoy with freedom that time which is not devoted to study, and may follow unmolested those strong impulses which Nature has wisely given for the furtherance of her benevolent purposes; but if, before her natural vivacity is entirely subdued by habit, little Miss is inclined to show her locomotive tricks in a manner not entirely agreeable to the trammels of custom, she is reproved with a sharpness which gives her a consciousness of having highly transgressed the laws of decorum; and what with the vigilance of those who are appointed to superintend her conduct, and the false bias they have imposed on her mind, every vigorous exertion is suppressed, the mind and body yield to the tyranny of error, and Nature is charged with all those imperfections which we alone owe to the blunders of art. [...]

There is another prejudice, Hortensia, which affects yet more deeply female happiness and female importance; a prejudice which ought ever to have been confined to the regions of the east, because [it accords with the][9] state of slavery to which female nature in that part of the world has been ever subjected, and can only suit with the notion of a positive inferiority in the intellectual powers of the female mind. You will soon perceive that the prejudice which I mean is that degrading difference in the culture of the understanding, which has prevailed for several centuries in all European societies. Our ancestors, on the first revival of letters, dispensed with an equal hand the advantages of a classical education to all their offspring; but as pedantry was the fault of that age, a female student might not at that time be a very agreeable character. True philosophy in those ages was rarely an attendant on learning, even in the male sex; but it must be obvious to all those who are not blinded by the mist of prejudice, that there is no cultivation which yields so promising a harvest as the cultivation of the understanding; and that a mind irradiated by the clear light of wisdom, must be equal to every task which reason imposes on it. The social duties in the interesting characters of daughter, wife and mother, will be but ill performed by ignorance and levity; and in the domestic converse of husband and wife, the alternative of an enlightened or an unenlightened companion, cannot be indifferent to any man of taste and true knowledge.

Be no longer niggards, then, O ye parents, in bestowing on your offspring every blessing which nature and fortune renders them capable of enjoying! Confine

---

[9] This phrase is missing from the text.

not the education of your daughters to what is regarded as the ornamental parts of it, nor deny the graces to your sons. Suffer no prejudices to prevail on you to weaken Nature in order to render her more beautiful; take measures for the virtue and the harmony of your family, by uniting their young minds early in the soft bonds of friendship. Let your children be brought up together; let their sports and studies be the same; let them enjoy, in the constant presence of those who are set over them, all that freedom which innocence renders harmless, and in which Nature rejoices. By the uninterrupted intercourse which you will thus establish, both sexes will find that friendship may be enjoyed between them without passion. The wisdom of your daughters will preserve them from the bane of coquetry, and even at the age of desire, objects of temptation will lose somewhat of their stimuli, by losing their novelty. Your sons will look for something more solid in women than a mere outside; and be no longer the dupes to the meanest, the weakest, and the most profligate of the sex. They will become the constant benefactors of that part of their family who stand in need of their assistance; and in regard to all matters of domestic concern, the unjust distinction of primogeniture will be deprived of its sting.

Letter XXII: No Characteristic Difference in Sex

The great difference that is observable in the characters of the sexes, Hortensia, as they display themselves in the scenes of social life, has given rise to much false speculation on the natural qualities of the female mind. For though the doctrine of innate ideas, and innate affections, are [sic] in a great measure exploded by the learned,[10] yet few persons reason so closely and so accurately on abstract subjects as, through a long chain of deductions, to bring forth a conclusion which in no respect militates with their premises.

It is a long time before the crowd give up opinions they have been taught to look upon with respect; and I know many persons who will follow you willingly through the course of your argument, till they perceive it tends to the overthrow of some fond prejudice; and then they will either sound a retreat, or begin a contest in which the contender for truth, though he cannot be overcome, is effectually silenced, from the mere weariness of answering positive assertions, reiterated without end. It is from such causes that the notion of a sexual difference in the human character has, with a very few exceptions, universally prevailed from the earliest times, and the pride of one sex and the ignorance and vanity of the other, have helped to support an opinion which a close observation of Nature, and a more accurate way of reasoning, would disprove.

It must be confessed that the virtues of the males among the human species,

[10] This is a reference to John Locke's *Essay Concerning Human Understanding*.

though mixed and blended with a variety of vices and errors, have displayed a bolder and a more consistent picture of excellence than female nature has hitherto done. It is on these reasons that, when we compliment the appearance of a more than ordinary energy in the female mind, we call it masculine; and hence it is, that Pope has elegantly said *a perfect woman's but a softer man*.[11] And if we take in the consideration that there can be but one rule of moral excellence for beings made of the same materials, organized after the same manner, and subjected to similar laws of Nature, we must either agree with Mr Pope, or we must reverse the proposition and say that *a perfect man is a woman formed after a coarser mould*. The difference that actually does subsist between the sexes, is too flattering for me to be willingly imputed to accident; for what accident occasions, wisdom might correct; and it is better, says pride, to give up the advantages we might derive from the perfection of our fellow associates, than to own that Nature has been just in the equal distribution of her favours. These are the sentiments of the men; but mark how readily they are yielded to by the women; not from humility, I assure you, but merely to preserve with character those fond vanities on which they set their hearts. No: suffer them to idolize their persons, to throw away their life in the pursuit of trifles, and to indulge in the gratification of the meaner passions, and they will heartily join in the sentence of their degradation.

Among the most strenuous asserters of a sexual difference in character, Rousseau is the most conspicuous, both on account of that warmth of sentiment which distinguishes all his writings, and the eloquence of his compositions: but never did enthusiasm and the love of paradox, those enemies to philosophical disquisition, appear in more strong opposition to plain sense than in Rousseau's definition of this difference. He sets out with a supposition that Nature intended the subjection of the one sex to the other; that consequently there must be an inferiority of intellect in the subjected party; but as man is a very imperfect being, and apt to play the capricious tyrant, Nature, to bring things nearer to an equality, bestowed on the woman such attractive graces and such an insinuating address, as to turn the balance on the other scale. Thus Nature, in a giddy mood, recedes from her purposes, and subjects prerogative to an influence which must produce confusion and disorder in the system of human affairs. Rousseau saw this objection; and in order to obviate it, he has made up a moral person of the union of the two sexes, which for contradiction and absurdity outdoes every metaphysical riddle that was ever formed in the schools.[12] In short, it is not reason, it is not wit; it is pride and sensuality that

---

[11] This is a reference to a passage from Alexander Pope's *Essay on Woman*, which reads 'And yet, believe me, good as well as ill, | Woman's at best a Contradiction still. | Heav'n when it strives to polish all it can | Its last best work, but forms a softer Man.'

[12] Scholastic philosophy, which originated in the medieval monastic schools, was condemned for wasting time debating impossible metaphysical riddles.

speak in Rousseau, and in this instance has lowered the man of genius to the licentious pedant.

But whatever might be the wise purpose intended by Providence in such a disposition of things, certain it is that some degree of inferiority in point of corporal strength seems always to have existed between the two sexes; and this advantage, in the barbarous ages of mankind, was abused to such a degree as to destroy all the natural rights of the female species, and reduce them to a state of abject slavery. What accidents have contributed in Europe to better their condition, would not be to my purpose to relate; for I do not intend to give you a history of women; I mean only to trace the sources of their peculiar foibles and vices; and these I firmly believe to originate in situation and education only: for so little did a wise and just Providence intend to make the condition of slavery an unalterable law of female nature, that in the same proportion as the male sex have consulted the interest of their own happiness, they have relaxed in their tyranny over women; and such is their use in the system of mundane creation, and such their natural influence over the male mind, that were these advantages properly exerted, they might carry every point of any importance to their honour and happiness. However, till that period arrives in which women will act wisely, we will amuse ourselves in talking of their follies.

The situation and education of women, Hortensia, is precisely that which must necessarily tend to corrupt and debilitate both the powers of mind and body. From a false notion of beauty and delicacy, their system of nerves is depraved before they come out of their nursery; and this kind of depravity has more influence over the mind, and consequently over morals, than is commonly apprehended. But it would be well if such causes only acted towards the debasement of the sex; their moral education is, if possible, more absurd than their physical. The principles and nature of virtue, which is never properly explained to boys, is kept quite a mystery to girls. They are told indeed that they must abstain from those vices which are contrary to their personal happiness, or they will be regarded as criminals, both by God and man; but all the higher parts of rectitude, everything that ennobles our being, and that renders us both innocuous and useful, is either not taught, or is taught in such a manner as to leave no proper impression on the mind. This is so obvious a truth that the defects of female education have ever been a fruitful topic of declamation for the moralist; but not one of this class of writers have laid down any judicious rules for amendment. Whilst we still retain the absurd notion of a sexual excellence, it will militate against the perfecting a plan of education for either sex. The judicious Addison[13] animadverts on the absurdity of bringing a young lady up

---

[13] Joseph Addison (1672–1719) was the editor of the *Spectator* magazine, which ran from 1711 to 1714; he wrote many of its articles himself, and was admired for his judgment and his style.

with no higher idea of the end of education than to make her agreeable to a husband, and confining the necessary excellence for this happy acquisition to the mere graces of person.

Every parent and tutor may not express himself in the same manner as is marked out by Addison; yet certain it is that the admiration of the other sex is held out to women as the highest honour they can attain; and whilst this is considered as their *summum bonum*,[14] and the beauty of their persons the chief *desideratum*[15] of men, Vanity, and its companion Envy, must taint, in their characters, every native and every acquired excellence. Nor can you, Hortensia, deny that these qualities, when united to ignorance, are fully equal to the engendering and riveting all those vices and foibles which are peculiar to the female sex; vices and foibles which have caused them to be considered in ancient times as beneath cultivation, and in modern days have subjected them to the censure and ridicule of writers of all descriptions, from the deep thinking philosopher to the man of ton[16] and gallantry, who by the by, sometimes distinguishes himself by qualities which are not greatly superior to those he despises in women.

Nor can I better illustrate the truth of this observation than by the following picture, to be found in the polite and gallant Chesterfield.[17] 'Women', says his Lordship, 'are only children of a larger growth. They have an entertaining tattle, sometimes wit; but for solid reasoning and good sense, I never in my life knew one that had it, or who acted or reasoned in consequence of it for four and twenty hours together. A man of sense only trifles with them, plays with them, humours and flatters them, as he does an engaging child; but he neither consults them, nor trusts them in serious matters.'[18]

---

[14] The highest good.
[15] The thing to be desired.
[16] 'Ton' was a French word that conveyed a sense of social sophistication.
[17] Philip Stanhope (1694–1773), 4th Earl of Chesterfield, wrote a series of letters of advice to his son that were published after his death. His cynical and world-weary style and emphasis on manners rather than morals were found offensive by many readers, and Macaulay's description of him as 'polite and gallant' may be regarded as ironic.
[18] Lord Chesterfield, *Letters to his Son*, 2 vols (London: J. Dodsley, 1774), I, pp. 330–31.

— 7 —
Maurice de Talleyrand

The crisis of the French Revolution shook the foundations of European thought. When the Revolution began in July 1789 with the capture of the Bastille, many people in Britain assumed it would resemble the events in America, where the colonists, having achieved their independence, established a liberal Constitution and were content to fight their battles through legal and political means. The executions of the king and queen and the Reign of Terror shocked and horrified them, and a week later France declared war on Britain: a war that (with a brief truce in 1802–03) was not to end until the final defeat of Napoleon in 1815.

The Declaration of the Rights of Man was passed by the French National Assembly in August 1789, and the ambiguous use of the term 'man' to refer either to the male sex or to the human race in general opened a route for women to claim that they also had rights, and needed to be liberated from the despotism not only of kings but of all men. As it soon turned out, this was not at all what the revolutionary leaders had in mind.

The Constitution introduced the concept of 'active' and 'passive' citizens: only male property owners over the age of twenty-five qualified as active citizens and could vote or hold public office. This limited the voting franchise to around four million men, and excluded women along with children and servants. A group of women presented a petition to the National Assembly demanding that women should have the right to be appointed as magistrates and elected to the regional and national assemblies. (It also suggested that wearing breeches should no longer be the prerogative of the male sex, which may have detracted from its perceived seriousness.)

A further demand for women's rights came from the playwright Olympe de Gouges (1748–1793), whose own education was so poor that she was barely literate and had to dictate her works to a secretary. In September 1791 she published a *Declaration of the Rights of Women & the Female Citizen*,[1] demanding that the women of France should be given their own national assembly, since the sole cause of all public ills and governmental corruption was historic contempt for the 'sacred and inalienable rights of women'. It called for women to form

---

[1] Olympe de Gouges, *Déclaration des Droits de la Femme et de la Citoyenne*, 1791.

political associations, choose their own representatives, and be free to appeal to the law against injustice or oppression (thus ending the authority of husbands over their wives). This document was firmly ignored and a new constitution promulgated which made it explicit that women did not and could not share in the rights of citizenship.

The Assembly set up a committee to look into the possibility of creating a system of state education, and in September 1791, the same month that De Gouges's *Déclaration* was published, the Marquis de Talleyrand presented its recommendations. The report had 220 pages, of which precisely six were dedicated to the education of women.

Charles-Maurice de Talleyrand-Périgord (1754–1838) was the greatest political survivor of his time. Born into an aristocratic family and disqualified from a military career because of his club foot, he sought to make his fame and fortune through the Church. Six months before the Revolution he was consecrated as Bishop of Autun, and he attended the Estates General as a representative of the clergy. To general amazement, he sided with the anti-clerical principles of the revolutionaries, supporting the confiscation of Church properties and participating in the drafting of the *Declaration of the Rights of Man*. On the first anniversary of the fall of the Bastille, he celebrated Mass at an enormous open-air celebration, and his reward was to be excommunicated by the pope.

Talleyrand was to turn his coat several more times in the future, not only surviving but amassing great wealth and holding important posts under Napoleon, the restored monarch Louis XVIII and the Orléanist king Louis Philippe. In 1791, however, he was apparently a sincere supporter of the Revolution and an easy choice to chair the Committee on Public Education.

The Committee's report illustrates the awkwardness faced by a group of men who, having publicly declared that liberty and equality were key principles of the Republic, had to find an acceptable justification for keeping women in the same social position they had occupied for centuries. They found it in the doctrine of public utility, claiming that it was not only good for society but also for women themselves that they should be confined to a domestic setting and taught only such skills as were necessary for them to fulfil their allotted role.

The beginning of the paper is clearly addressed to the middle class, who could afford to keep their daughters at home and employ suitable tutors. However, it must have been drawn to the attention of the legislators that many families relied on women's work to survive, and they inserted a proposal to provide a substitute for those convent schools run by the Church that the Revolution had abolished, in the form of institutions established under state supervision to train for manual trades those girls who could not rely on male economic support.

The legislators were familiar with the principles of their hero Rousseau, whose ashes would in 1794 be reverently transferred to the Panthéon in Paris, the 'Temple of the Nation'. The exclusively domestic destiny of women is described not only as necessary for the common good but as prescribed by the will of Nature, who distributes clearly distinct functions to the two sexes. Preserving this distinction is not merely a matter of public utility but a 'sacred duty'.

If a woman attempted to throw off these state-sanctioned restrictions during the French Revolution, it could lead to her execution. One such was Manon Roland (1754–1793), born Marie-Jeanne Phlipon, the only surviving child of a Parisian engraver. Her mother was determined to train her for a future as a wife and mother but she was a voracious reader, and later claimed that by the age of nine she had finished all thirteen volumes of Plutarch's *Lives of the Greeks & Romans*, leaving her with distinctly anti-monarchist views and an admiration for the heroic republican virtues. She read the works of Voltaire, and a friend once warned her mother to take care she didn't turn into a *savante*.[2] She also became an admirer of Rousseau, not only his writings on political liberty, but also *Julie* and the emotionally intense *Confessions*.[3] At the age of twenty-three, she submitted an essay for a prize offered by the Academy of Besancon on the subject 'How the education of women could contribute to the improvement of men'; this conveyed the conventional message that women's destiny is to make men happy, and was entirely consistent with Rousseau's views as expressed in *Émile*.

In March 1792 Manon's husband Jean-Marie Roland was appointed Minister of the Interior, and she found herself at the centre of power. The couple moved into a magnificent Parisian mansion, and Manon arranged for the Council of Ministers to dine with them every Friday, so matters of state were discussed in her presence; no other woman was ever invited. The extent of her influence over her husband was quickly observed; petitioners would present their requests to her on the pretext of leaving a message for the minister, in the knowledge that he would consult her anyway. She acted as his private secretary and drafted all his important documents.

When the Jacobins took control of the National Assembly, they gave free rein to their detestation of women who did not know their place. Madame Roland was accused of treasonous correspondence with royalist *émigrés* and slandered in the press. One article, littered with obscenities, described her circle as a new court, with Manon wallowing in luxury and dispensing sexual favours to the men around her. The writer claimed he had seen twenty chefs delivering trays of delicacies to Madame Roland's banquets, and asserted that she was seducing

---

[2] The masculine noun *savant* means a scholar or learned man. The feminine equivalent had already become a term of mockery, denoting a woman who has memorised scholarly terminology without really understanding it. Molière's popular 1672 play *Les Femmes Savantes* made fun of silly women who have pretensions to be learned.

[3] Jean-Jacques Rousseau, *Confessions* (Geneva: n.pub., 1782 & 1789).

all the men with her charms but at the same time was a bald, toothless old hag.[4] She was arrested on 31 October 1793, and after a brief show-trial sent to the guillotine.

A week after her death, an anonymous article in the *Moniteur* made it clear that Roland had to die not only as a political opponent but as a woman who had favoured education over domesticity:

> The Roland woman, a would-be wit with great plans, a philosopher who wrote billet-doux, the queen of a moment [...] was a monster in every respect [...] She was a mother, but had sacrificed her nature by wanting to raise herself above it. The desire to be learned caused her to forget the duties of her sex, and this neglect, always dangerous, finally led her to perish on the scaffold.[5]

Five days before the execution of Manon Roland, the irrepressible Olympe de Gouges had also gone to the guillotine. The Commune's prosecutor described her offence in almost the same words: she died not merely for treason or conspiracy, but for stepping outside her prescribed sphere. This should be a warning to all women.

> Remember that virago, that man-woman, the impertinent Olympe de Gouges, who was the first to set up women's societies, who abandoned all her domestic duties, wanted to play at politics and committed crimes [...] It was forgetting her sex that led her to the scaffold [...] All these immoral creatures have been obliterated by the avenging blade: and you wish to imitate them? No, you will come to realise that you will not be of interest and truly worthy of esteem until you are what nature wished you to be. We wish women to be respected, and that is why we shall force them to respect themselves.[6]

As the Revolution progressed, the war against those rights which women had been granted in its early idealistic days continued. In September 1794, a debate was held in the Convention to consider whether women's civic rights should be repealed. Jean-Pierre-André Amar, one of the Jacobin *députés*, expressed his opinion as follows:

> We have to say that this question is essentially a moral one, and without morals there is no Republic. Does a respectable woman show herself in public and dispute with men, and debate in front of the people questions on which the safety of the Republic depend? Generally speaking, women are incapable of profound concepts and serious considerations; and if in the nations of antiquity their natural timidity and modesty did not permit them to appear outside their homes, do you desire that in the French

---

[4] Jacques Hébert in *Le Pere Duchesne* No. 202, December 1792.
[5] *Le Moniteur*, November 1793.
[6] Pierre-Gaspard Chaumette, cited in Olivier Blanc, *Olympe de Gouges, des Droits de la Femme à la Guillotine* (Paris: Tallandier, 2014), p. 227.

Republic we should see them appear at the bar, on the podium, in political assemblies alongside men, abandoning all decorum, the source of all the virtues of their sex, and neglecting their families?[7]

Talleyrand's recommendation to the National Assembly that girls should be educated at home may have been unexceptional for its time, but in the fervour of the Revolution a woman courted not only social disapproval but violent death if she indulged a 'desire to be learned' and stepped outside her allotted sphere.

❖

Maurice de Talleyrand-Périgord
Report on Public Education made to the National Assembly
10–19 September 1791
(Paris: Baudouin & Du Pont, 1791)

We announced at the beginning of our work some principles for the education of women: these principles appear to us to be very simple.

First, one cannot separate the questions regarding their education from the examination of their political rights: for in training them it is necessary to know for what they are destined. If we accord them the same rights as men, we need to give them the same means to deploy such rights. If we think that their role should be solely domestic happiness and the duties of the home, we must train them from an early age to fulfil this destiny. [...]

The aim of all institutions should be the happiness of the greatest number. Anything that diverges from this is an error, and anything that leads to it is a truth. If the exclusion from public employment pronounced against women is for the two sexes a method to increase the sum of their mutual happiness, it is henceforth a law that all societies should recognise and consider sacred. Any other ambition would be a reversal of the primary destinies, and women will never have any interest in changing the part allotted to them.

Now it seems to us incontestable that the common good, particularly that of women, demands that they do not aspire to exercise political rights and functions. We seek their interest in this case in the will of Nature. Is it not evident that their delicate constitutions, their peaceful inclinations and the many duties of motherhood, keep them firmly separated from difficult habits and painful duties, and call them to gentle occupations and domestic tasks? And how could we not see that the principal preserver of societies, which have identified harmony as relying on the division of powers, has been explained and indeed revealed by Nature, when she distributed to the two sexes functions that are so evidently distinct? Let us stick to this, and not invoke principles that

---

[7] Cited in Florence Lotterie, *Le Genre des Lumières: Femme et philosophe au XVIIIe siècle* (Paris: Classiques Garnier, 2013), p. 252.

are inapplicable to this question. Do not turn your life companions into rivals: permit a union to exist in this world that no interest and no competitive feeling can break. You must believe that the good of all demands this of you.

Far from the tumult of affairs, ah! how beautiful is the role in life allotted to women! The office of motherhood, that emotion which no one can yet claim to have adequately expressed in words, is a solitary joy that would be distracted by public responsibilities; to leave to women that power of love that other passions would weaken, is this not above all to have concern for their life's happiness?

It is said that in important situations, women have strengthened the character of men, but that is because they were not competing in the same race. If they had pursued the same glory, they would have lost the right to distribute the prizes.

It is also said that several women have held the sceptre to great effect, but what matters a small number of brilliant exceptions? Do these authorise us to distort the general plan of nature? If there were still a few women who by the accidents of their education or their talents appeared to be called to the same existence as a man, they should sacrifice this to the welfare of the majority, showing their superiority over their sex in judgment and indicating to them their true place. They should not demand that by admitting women to the same studies as us, we sacrifice the whole sex in order to create a few more men in the course of a century.

Let us not seek any further to find a solution to a problem that is satisfactorily resolved; let us train women, not to aspire to advantages that the Constitution refuses them, but to recognise and appreciate those it guarantees them: instead of making them despise the portion of well-being that society reserves to them in exchange for the important services it requires of them, let us teach them that this is the true measure of their duties and of their rights. May they find not chimerical hopes but real benefits under the empire of liberty and equality; may they know that the less they compete in the creation of the law, the more they will receive from its protection and strength; and above all that at the moment when they renounce all political rights, they acquire the certainty of seeing their civil rights confirmed and even increased.

Since they are assured of such an existence by the legal system, it is necessary to prepare them for it by their education; but let us develop their faculties without denaturing them, and may their apprenticeship for life be to them a school of both happiness and virtue.

Men are destined to live in the theatre of the world. Public education is appropriate for them: it puts before them at an early age all the scenes of life, and only the proportions are different. The family home is a better place for the education of women; they have less need to learn to deal with the interests of others than to become accustomed to a calm and retired life. Destined for domestic tasks, it is in the bosom of their family that they should receive their first lessons and their first examples. Fathers and mothers, alert to this sacred duty, will be aware of the extent of the obligations it imposes on them, for the presence of a young girl purifies the place she inhabits, and innocence requires of all around it either repentance or virtue. May all your institutions therefore aim to concentrate female education within this domestic retreat: there is none more suitable to modesty, and which prepares them better for the most delicate way of life.

But the foresight of the law, having recommended the best type of education, must also prepare resources for exceptions and remedies for suffering. The fatherland must also be a tender and vigilant mother. Before the cancellation of monastic vows, a multitude of religious houses, created with this intention, attracted young people of both sexes towards public education. This general direction was not a good thing, for these establishments were in no way appropriate to train wives and mothers. But they did at least offer an asylum for innocence, and it is indispensable to replace this advantage. We shall have no reason to regret the loss of convent education, but we would rightly regret their protective existence if other institutions equally reassuring and better managed did not rise in their place.

Each Department[8] must therefore take care to establish a sufficient number of such establishments, and assign to them schoolmistresses whose virtue will be sufficient to guarantee public confidence. The women who will dedicate themselves to such a delicate duty will not take vows, but they will enter into commitments towards Society that are all the more sacred for being freely given, and will produce the same effect for the security of families.

In these houses young girls will find all the resources necessary for their education, and especially the apprenticeship to different trades that may assure them a livelihood.

Until the age of eight there can be no objection to their attending primary schools, and learning there the elements that should be common to both sexes; but before they move beyond childhood they must withdraw and enclose themselves in the family home, in the knowledge that official institutions are an imperfect replacement for this. It is at this point that we must procure other resources to teach them useful skills and give them the means to live an independent life by the product of their labour.

Therefore, taking the terms of the Constitution as our guide, we recommend home education for women as being the most appropriate to prepare them for the virtues that they must acquire. In the absence of this advantage, we shall establish institutions under the inspection of the Departments, and facilitate their apprenticeship to the trades appropriate to their sex.

---

[8] The revolutionary government had divided France into administrative Departments.

— 8 —
Mary Wollstonecraft

Mary Wollstonecraft was born in London in 1759, the second of seven children. Her family was originally comfortably off, but her father squandered their money by unsuccessful attempts to become a gentleman farmer. This did, however, have the advantage that she spent part of her childhood in the Yorkshire countryside and was able to run around in freedom, as Rousseau had recommended.

Mary's father sometimes compensated for his professional disappointments by beating his wife in drunken rages, and from an early age she demonstrated a desire to defend women against unreasonable men by trying to protect her mother from his attacks. She received little formal education, but formed a friendship with a young woman who lived nearby, and was able to escape from her own dysfunctional family by reading books with her and listening to her father talk about science and literature.

Her family's penury meant that Mary could not live the life of a lady but had to earn her own living. At the age of nineteen she worked as companion to a widow living in Bath, then she and her sisters set up a school in Newington Green in London, but it struggled to attract pupils. Mary was by now in desperate financial straits, and eagerly accepted the offer of a substantial advance of £10 from the publisher Joseph Johnson to write a book on education. The result was *Thoughts on the Education of Daughters*, a short anonymous work in which only the first sixty pages were actually on the subject, with the rest covering such subjects as love, matrimony and how to treat your servants. The book expressed approval of Rousseau's approach to education — the one proposed for Émile rather than for Sophie — for she believed the mind should be 'put into a proper train, and then left to itself [...] the mind is not, cannot be created by the teacher, though it may be cultivated, and its real powers found out'.[1] She did not recommend any particular curriculum for girls, but made it clear that they should be taught to think. She was not opposed to 'accomplishments' like dancing as long as they were not taken to excess, did not approve of works which encourage an affectation of sensibility and insisted that

---

[1] Mary Wollstonecraft, *Thoughts on the Education of Daughters, with reflections on female conduct in the more important duties of life* (London: J. Johnson, 1787), p. 54.

studying was not incompatible with women's domestic duties.

After an unsuccessful episode as a governess in Ireland, Mary took the remarkable decision to become a professional writer. She moved back to London and applied to Joseph Johnson for a job: impressed by such boldness, he set her up in a house rent-free, and agreed that she would repay him through her writing. She started by writing book reviews for Johnson's literary and scientific journal *The Analytical Review*; this was aimed not at specialists but at the general public, with the intention of spreading knowledge of the works of Continental writers. Johnson's shop became a venue for impassioned debate between young radicals who believed society needed to undergo significant reform, and Mary was able to join in this exhilarating intellectual exchange.

During her time at Newington Green, Mary had become associated with a group surrounding the Unitarian minister Richard Price. Price and his congregation were Dissenters, descendants of the many nonconformist groups established during the Commonwealth period. As such, they were officially discriminated against, and were not allowed to enter parliament, hold public office, serve in the military or attend university. Mary had become a member of a group of social and political outsiders.

In November 1790, Price preached a sermon in support of the French Revolution. This led to a counterblast from Edmund Burke, who published *Reflections on the Revolution in France*,[2] condemning the revolutionaries and lauding the British constitution and social order. Burke defended hierarchy, rank and property, and was alarmed at suggestions that the poor should be encouraged to leave their subordinate position.

Mary's reaction to Burke's *Reflections* was one of furious indignation with his complacent approval of the state of contemporary British society. Johnson encouraged her to write a response, and within a month she rushed out a short work entitled *A Vindication of the Rights of Men*,[3] with Johnson printing the pages as she wrote them. It was largely a personal attack on Burke, condemning him for believing that just because something is old it must therefore be good. Her most passionate diatribes were attacks on hereditary property and appeals for the support of the poor. The book was sufficiently popular that Johnson quickly brought out a second edition with Mary's name on the title-page: she was now officially an author.

The following year, Johnson encouraged her to follow up this success with a book on women's rights, and she set off at her usual furious pace, producing within six weeks a 450-page volume entitled *A Vindication of the Rights of*

---

[2] Edmund Burke, *Reflections on the Revolution in France* (London: J. Dodsley, 1790).
[3] Mary Wollstonecraft, *A Vindication of the Rights of Men, in a Letter to the Right Honourable Edmund Burke* (London: J. Johnson, 1790).

Woman.[4] The book argued that society must be completely re-ordered, not just improved or reformed: hierarchies must be abolished and society made more egalitarian. Mary dedicated the book to Maurice de Talleyrand, in the knowledge that he had proposed to the French Assembly a new system of state education. (It seems that she may not have read this document carefully, given the restrictions it put on the education of girls.) Talleyrand visited London shortly after the *Vindication* was published, and out of curiosity paid a visit to Mary, whom he found to be exactly the kind of shabbily dressed and emotionally excitable bluestocking he had imagined, and was taken aback when she served him wine in cracked teacups.

A substantial part of the *Vindication* consists of an unbridled attack on Rousseau's views on women. Wollstonecraft acknowledges the faults in the contemporary female character, but asserts that these have been deliberately caused by men, who have set out to make women their slaves by keeping them foolish and ignorant, and quotes the statement in *Émile* that 'with respect to the female character, obedience is the grand lesson which ought to be impressed with unrelenting rigour'. The servile position enforced on women enrages her:

> Gentleness, docility, and a spaniel-like affection are [...] consistently recommended as the cardinal virtues of the sex [...] She was created to be the toy of man, his rattle, and it must jingle in his ears whenever, dismissing reason, he chooses to be amused.[5]

It is proper education that will enable women to appreciate the injustice of their position; men refuse it to them in order to keep them as 'insignificant objects of desire'. They resist educating women since they know that if the female mind is strengthened women will rebel against their servitude, and 'there will be an end of blind obedience'.

Wollstonecraft rejects other women's admiration for Rousseau: she was conscious of his contradictions, saying 'Who ever drew a more exalted female character than Rousseau? though in the lump he constantly endeavoured to degrade the sex', and was concerned that they failed to see the pernicious effect of his praise for women's sexual charms:

> The master wished to have a meretricious slave to fondle, entirely dependent on his reason and bounty; he did not want a companion, whom he should be compelled to esteem, or a friend to whom her could confide the care of his children's education [...] He denies woman reason, shuts her out from knowledge, and turns her aside from truth, yet his pardon is granted, because 'he admits the passion of love'.[6]

---

[4] Mary Wollstonecraft, *A Vindication of the Rights of Woman, with Strictures on Moral and Political Subjects* (London: J. Johnson, 1792).
[5] Wollstonecraft, *Vindication*, p. 66.
[6] Wollstonecraft, *Vindication*, p. 231.

Wollstonecraft quotes Rousseau's statement that if women are educated like men, 'the more they resemble our sex the less power will they have over us', and declares that 'I do not wish them to have power over men; but over themselves' and 'it is not empire, but equality, that they should contend for'. She is conscious that beauty is fleeting, and if 'women are kept from the tree of knowledge, the important years of youth, the usefulness of age, and the rational hopes of futurity, are all to be sacrificed to render women an object of desire for a *short time*'.

Wollstonecraft also gives James Fordyce a place in her gallery of shame, finding his cloying praise for women as angels and sweet innocents rather revolting, and describing his sermons as a 'sentimental rant'. She particularly objects to his infantilisation of women, who are not expected to develop beyond a state of helpless dependence, and finds the pedestal which Fordyce puts them on to be a trap rather than an honour, asking 'Why are girls to be told that they resemble angels; but to sink them below women?' She dismisses a whole range of male conduct book writers with the words: 'The pernicious tendency of those books, in which the writers insidiously degrade the sex whilst they are prostrate before their personal charms, cannot be too often or too severely exposed'.

Wollstonecraft tackles the question of whether women are capable of sustained reasoning, and quotes Rousseau's view that 'researches into abstract and speculative truths, the principles and axioms of sciences, in short, every thing that tends to generalize our ideas, is not the proper province of women'. By contrast, she has no doubt that women have the same abilities as men but are deliberately and unjustly denied the opportunity to practise rigorous intellectual analysis. To her this is not a small point, but a central defining human characteristic: with a direct reference to the theories of John Locke, she states that 'the power of generalizing ideas, of drawing comprehensive conclusions from individual observations, is the only acquirement, for an immortal being, that really deserves the name of knowledge'. The opportunity to develop this basic human function has been deliberately withheld from women, on the specious grounds that it is inconsistent with their sexual character. Her conclusion is that 'the mother, who wishes to give true dignity of character to her daughter, must, regardless of the sneers of ignorance, proceed on a plan diametrically opposite to that which Rousseau has recommended'.

The *Vindication* was an immediate bestseller and was re-reprinted within months; two American editions and a French translation appeared in the same year, and translations into German and Italian soon followed. Most of the London reviews were coolly favourable, but the Boston newspaper the *Columbian Centinel* enthused that Wollstonecraft's spirit, 'agonized at the lordly degradation of Woman, has entered the lists of literary combat, against hoary prejudices, whose antique features have long since rendered them respectable personages: and it must be acknowledged she weilds [sic] the sword of reason, with the dexterity of a scientifick warriour'.[7]

However, there was already a groundswell of opposition. Hannah More refused even to read the *Vindication of the Rights of Woman*, stating that she found the very title ridiculous.[8] She later rejected the whole concept of rights: in her world view, society was held together by a hierarchical chain of duties and obligations. What nonsense would appear next, she mused, the rights of children, or the rights of babies?[9]

Wollstonecraft intended to write a second part to the *Vindication*, but her life was about to become very complicated. She travelled to France to observe the Revolution first-hand, but was caught up in the Terror and escaped prison only with the help of her lover Gilbert Imlay, who promptly abandoned her and their daughter. Wollstonecraft struggled back to London, where in desperation she attempted to commit suicide. She then travelled to Scandinavia, accompanied only by a servant and her young child, in an attempt to recover a commercial debt owed to Imlay. On her return, she started a novel, entitled *Maria, or the Wrongs of Woman*, in which she defended women's right to sexual freedom and attacked society's refusal to allow them proper employment. It attempts to view society from the point of view of poor and marginalised women: servants and even prostitutes. (Hannah More was particularly disgusted by its defence of a woman who had committed adultery.)

The book was never finished, for Mary had fallen in love again. The object of her passion on this occasion was William Godwin, a forty-year-old political theorist who had publicly stated his objections to the institution of marriage. They became lovers, and he compromised his principles sufficiently to marry her when she became pregnant. Following the birth of their daughter Mary fell victim to the age-old danger of childbirth and contracted septicaemia, dying ten days later.

Godwin was devastated by her loss, and rashly proceeded to publish a biography of his late wife which disclosed that she had lived with Imlay and later with himself out of wedlock, and had borne an illegitimate child.[10] He also described her suicide attempts. As a result, Mary Wollstonecraft and her works were rejected with horror and all mention of her banished from polite society. Conservative journals such as the *Anti-Jacobin Review* seized on the *Memoirs* with glee and exaggerated Mary's faults to present her as a model of depravity,

---

[7] *Columbian Centinel*, Boston, November 28, 1792.
[8] Letter from Hannah More to Horace Walpole, 1793, in *Memoirs of the Life & Correspondence of Mrs Hannah More*, ed. by Roberts, II, p. 371.
[9] More, *Strictures on Female Education*, 2 vols (London: T. Cadell & W. Davies, 1800), 8th edn, I, p. 173.
[10] William Godwin, *Memoirs of the Author of A Vindication of the Rights of Woman* (London: J. Johnson, 1798).

overtly labelling her a prostitute. The *European Magazine* pronounced that Godwin's *Memoirs* were to be read:

> with disgust by every female who has any pretensions to delicacy; with detestation by every one attached to the interests of religion and morality, and with indignation by anyone who might feel any regard for the unhappy woman, whose frailties should have been buried in oblivion.[11]

Seven years later, the conservative writer Jane West crowed triumphantly:

> I have quoted from a book which, by supereminent absurdity and audacity, exposed the principles that it meant to support to profound contempt. It indeed amazed and confounded for a day; and it received all the assistance which an elaborate analysis could bestow, to elevate it into lasting celebrity. It was soon found, however, that the times were not sufficiently illuminated to bear such strong doctrine; and the disciples of the school of equality have since found it more convenient to gloss and soften, and misrepresent.[12]

Despite these assurances of oblivion, the *Vindication* was not completely forgotten, and a heavily edited third edition was published in London in 1844. A further edition followed in 1891, with an introduction written by the suffragist leader Millicent Garrett Fawcett. However, even then it was regarded as an extremist publication and admired only by those who were seen as social revolutionaries. The 'irregularities' of Mary Wollstonecraft's life still detracted from public acceptance of her powerful arguments.

❖

Mary Wollstonecraft
A Vindication of the Rights of Woman
London: J. Johnson, 1792

The most perfect education, in my opinion, is such an exercise of the understanding as is best calculated to strengthen the body and form the heart. Or, in other words, to enable the individual to attain such habits of virtue as will render it independent. In fact, it is a farce to call any being virtuous whose virtues do not result from the exercise of its own reason. This was Rousseau's opinion respecting men: I extend it to women, and confidently assert that they have been drawn out of their sphere by false refinement, and not by an endeavour to acquire masculine qualities. Still the regal homage which they receive is so intoxicating that till the manners of the times are changed, and formed on more reasonable principles, it may be impossible to convince them

---

[11] *The European Magazine & London Review*, April 1798, p. 251.
[12] Jane West, *Letters to a Young Lady, in which the Duties and Character of Women are Considered, Chiefly with a Reference to Prevailing Opinions*, 3 vols (London: Longman, Hurst, Rees & Orme, 1806), I, p. 199.

that the illegitimate power which they obtain by degrading themselves is a curse, and that they must return to nature and equality, if they wish to secure the placid satisfaction that unsophisticated affections impart. But for this epoch we must wait — wait, perhaps, till kings and nobles, enlightened by reason, and preferring the real dignity of man to childish state, throw off their gaudy hereditary trappings: and if then women do not resign the arbitrary power of beauty — they will prove that they have *less* mind than man.

I may be accused of arrogance; still I must declare what I firmly believe, that all the writers who have written on the subject of female education and manners, from Rousseau to Dr Gregory,[13] have contributed to render women more artificial, weak characters than they would otherwise have been; and consequently, more useless members of society. I might have expressed this conviction in a lower key; but I am afraid it would have been the whine of affectation, and not the faithful expression of my feelings, of the clear result which experience and reflection have led me to draw. When I come to that division of the subject, I shall advert to the passages that I more particularly disapprove of in the works of the authors I have just alluded to; but it is first necessary to observe that my objection extends to the whole purport of those books, which tend, in my opinion, to degrade one half of the human species, and render women pleasing at the expense of every solid virtue. [...]

Many are the causes that, in the present corrupt state of society, contribute to enslave women by cramping their understandings and sharpening their sense. One, perhaps, that silently does more mischief than all the rest, is their disregard of order.

To do everything in an orderly manner is a most important precept which women, who generally speaking receive only a disorderly kind of education, seldom attend to with that degree of exactness that men, who from their infancy are broken into method, observe. This negligent kind of guess-work, for what other epithet can be used to point out the random exertions of a sort of instinctive common sense, never brought to the test of reason, prevents their generalizing matters of fact — so they do today what they did yesterday, merely because they did it yesterday.

This contempt of the understanding in early life has more baneful consequences than is commonly supposed: for the little knowledge which women of strong minds attain is, from various circumstances, of a more desultory kind than the knowledge of men, and it is acquired more by sheer observations on real life than from comparing what has been individually observed with the results of experience generalized by speculation.[14] Led by their dependent situation and

---

[13] Dr John Gregory was the author of *A Father's Legacy to his Daughters* (London: T. Cadell & W. Davies, 1774).
[14] This description of the nature of thought is derived from John Locke's *An Essay*

domestic employments more into society, what they learn is rather by snatches; and as learning is with them in general only a secondary thing, they do not pursue any one branch with that persevering ardour necessary to give vigour to the faculties, and clearness to the judgment. In the present state of society, a little learning is required to support the character of a gentleman; and boys are obliged to submit to a few years of discipline. But in the education of women, the cultivation of the understanding is always subordinate to the acquirement of some corporeal accomplishment; even while enervated by confinement and false notions of modesty, the body is prevented from attaining that grace and beauty which relaxed half-formed limbs never exhibit. Besides, in youth their faculties are not brought forward by emulation; and having no serious scientific study, if they have natural sagacity it is turned too soon on life and manners. They dwell on effects and modifications, without tracing them back to causes; and complicated rules to adjust behaviour are a weak substitute for simple principles. […]

I will allow that bodily strength seems to give man a natural superiority over woman; and this is the only solid basis on which the superiority of the sex can be built. But I still insist, that not only the virtue, but the *knowledge* of the two sexes should be the same in nature, if not in degree, and that women, considered not only as moral, but rational creatures, ought to endeavour to acquire human virtues (or perfections) by the same means as men, instead of being educated like a fanciful kind of half being — one of Rousseau's wild chimeras.[15]

But if strength of body be, with some show of reason, the boast of men, why are women so infatuated as to be proud of a defect? Rousseau has furnished them with a plausible excuse, which could only have occurred to a man whose imagination had been allowed to run wild, and refine on the impressions made by exquisite senses — that they might, forsooth, have a pretext for yielding to a natural appetite without violating a romantic species of modesty, which gratifies the pride and libertinism of man. […]

But should it be proved that woman is naturally weaker than man, whence does it follow that it is natural for her to become still weaker than nature intended her to be? Arguments of this cast are an insult to common sense, and savour of passion. The divine right of husbands, like the divine right of kings, may, it is to be hoped, in this enlightened age, be contested without danger, and though conviction may not silence many boisterous disputants, yet when any prevailing prejudice is attacked, the wise will consider, and leave the narrow-minded to rail with thoughtless vehemence at innovation.

Concerning Human Understanding.
[15] Here Wollstonecraft quotes in a footnote from Rousseau's *Émile*, 'Women have most wit, men have most genius; women observe, men reason.' The Chimera was a mythical monster composed of parts of different animals, usually a lion, a goat and a snake.

The mother who wishes to give true dignity of character to her daughter must, regardless of the sneers of ignorance, proceed on a plan diametrically opposite to that which Rousseau has recommended with all the deluding charms of eloquence and philosophical sophistry: for his eloquence renders absurdities plausible, and his dogmatic conclusions puzzle, without convincing, those who have not ability to refute them. [...]

I wish to sum up what I have said in a few words, for I here throw down my gauntlet, and deny the existence of sexual virtues, not excepting modesty. For man and woman, truth, if I understand the meaning of the word, must be the same; yet the fanciful female character so prettily drawn by poets and novelists, demanding the sacrifice of truth and sincerity, virtue becomes a relative idea, having no other foundation than utility, and of that utility men pretend arbitrarily to judge, shaping it to their own convenience.

Women, I allow, may have different duties to fulfil; but they are *human* duties, and the principles that should regulate the discharge of them, I sturdily maintain, must be the same.

To become respectable, the exercise of their understanding is necessary, there is no other foundation for independence of character; I mean explicitly to say that they must only bow to the authority of reason, instead of being the *modest* slaves of opinion. [...]

I have already inveighed against the custom of confining girls to their needle, and shutting them out from all political and civil employments; for by thus narrowing their minds they are rendered unfit to fulfil the peculiar duties which nature has assigned them.

Only employed about the little incidents of the day, they necessarily grow up cunning. My very soul has often sickened at observing the sly tricks practised by women to gain some foolish thing on which their silly hearts were set. Not allowed to dispose of money, or call anything their own, they learn to turn the market penny; or should a husband offend, by staying from home, or give rise to some emotions of jealousy — a new gown, or any pretty bauble, smooths Juno's angry brow.

But these *littlenesses* would not degrade their character if women were led to respect themselves, if political and moral subjects were opened to them; and I will venture to affirm that this is the only way to make them properly attentive to their domestic duties. An active mind embraces the whole circle of its duties, and finds time enough for all. It is not, I assert, a bold attempt to emulate masculine virtues; it is not the enchantment of literary pursuit, or the steady investigation of scientific subjects, that leads women astray from duty. No, it is indolence and vanity — the love of pleasure and the love of sway[16] — that

---

[16] A quotation from Alexander Pope's satirical poem *Epistle to a Lady, Of the Characters of Women*, 1743.

will reign paramount in an empty mind. I say empty emphatically, because the education which women now receive scarcely deserves the name.

— 9 —
Maria Edgeworth

Maria Edgeworth (1768–1849) had the opportunity to observe at close hand real-life experiments in the application of Rousseau's theories to the education of both boys and girls. Her father, Richard Edgeworth (1744–1817), was an enthusiastic inventor who married four times and had twenty-two children. He decided to bring up his eldest son Dick according to the principles set out in *Émile*: Dick was left to run barefoot around the fields and deliberately exposed to hunger, pain and fatigue. He was not taught to read books, instead spending his time at his father's side while he designed and manufactured his ingenious mechanical contraptions. By the time he was six years old he was hardy and independent — and completely uncontrollable. Edgeworth found he had created a little savage, and went to the opposite end of the scale by sending him to be educated by Oratorian priests at a French seminary known for its strict discipline. Dick left at the age of fifteen and joined the Royal Navy.

Maria was the next surviving child, born in 1768, and spent much of her life looking after her many brothers and sisters, the youngest of whom was forty-four years her junior. One of her father's best friends during her childhood was Thomas Day (1748–1789), whose unkempt appearance and overbearing manner made it difficult for him to persuade any of the women he knew to marry him; he concluded that they were all corrupted by modern society, and conceived the remarkable idea of adopting a young girl and bringing her up exactly like Rousseau's Sophie.[1] He and a friend persuaded the trustees of two orphanages to let them take away two girls on the spurious grounds that they were to be bound to Richard Edgeworth as servants: in fact they went to live with Day and were subjected to his strict interpretation of Rousseau's theories. One girl was found unsatisfactory and sent to another household, while the other was made to wait on Day as a servant while being obliged to suffer various tests of her compliance, such as having hot wax dripped on her arm. She did not in fact become his wife, but lived into old age as the housekeeper of a boys' school in London run by the brother of Fanny Burney, while Day married a self-sacrificing female of his own class.

---

[1] The story is described in detail in Wendy Moore's *How to Create the Perfect Wife* (London: Weidenfeld & Nicolson, 2013).

Maria was spared this sort of experimentation and given a conventional female upbringing at boarding schools in Derby and London. At the age of fourteen she returned home to her family's property in Ireland, where her father tutored her in politics, science, literature, law and economics, and she became his assistant in running the estate. Except for a period in 1802–03 when they travelled round Europe together, she remained there for the rest of her life, and Ireland was the inspiration for a series of novels and moral tales that she wrote over a period of thirty-four years, starting with *Castle Rackrent* in 1800. These books were highly popular, and until she was overtaken by Walter Scott she was for many years the best-selling British novelist.

In 1798, Maria published *Practical Education*,[2] officially a collaboration with her father and based on her extensive experience of teaching her own brothers and sisters. It was a progressive work that adopted the more sensible ideas of Rousseau and John Locke, arguing that children should be encouraged to adopt the discipline of learning rather than forced to memorise information, and including original and useful educational materials. It made no significant distinction between the basic education of girls and boys.

Three years before this, Maria had published a short and witty work entitled *Letters for Literary Ladies*,[3] a fictional exchange of correspondence inspired by letters that passed between her father and Thomas Day. Richard Edgeworth had asked his daughter to translate Madame de Genlis's *Adèle et Théodore*, but the project was aborted when a rival translation was published, and Day had written to Edgeworth to congratulate him on his daughter's narrow escape from the dangerous world of female authorship.

In Maria's version, the first gentleman writes to his friend congratulating him on the birth of a daughter and warning him against giving her a 'literary' education. He makes the remarkable claim to his friend that 'you are a champion for the rights of woman, and insist upon the equality of the sexes', but states that this would be against the interests of both the individual and society. Maria has some fun reflecting the restrictive views of people like Day, but if the statements she puts into the gentleman's mouth are compared with other contemporary texts in this collection, it will be seen that she is not taking her satire to an extreme.

The father of the newborn girl replies in what we may interpret as the tones of the author's father: he hastens to deny that he is a champion for the rights of woman, and sets out a justification for women's education that the average British gentleman might find acceptable. He reassures his correspondent that

---

[2] Maria Edgeworth and Richard Lovell Edgeworth, *Practical Education* (London: J. Johnson, 1798).
[3] Maria Edgeworth, *Letters for Literary Ladies, to which is added, an Essay on the Noble Science of Self-Justification* (London: J. Johnson, 1795).

educated women will not turn into overbearing pedants, and regards it as impossible that women will ever play a part in public affairs. He describes the pleasure experienced by men who enjoy 'union with women who can sympathize in all their thoughts and feelings, who can converse with them as equals, and live with them as friends; who can assist them in the important and delightful duty of educating their children; who can make their family their most agreeable society, and their home the attractive centre of happiness'. The benefits of educating women are here defined entirely by reference to their effect on men; it seems that the objective of reconciling women to their role as wives and mothers is the same as in Rousseau's *Émile*, but without the requirement to keep them in profound ignorance.

In the final passage of this extract, Edgeworth attacks Rousseau's praise of coquetry as natural and attractive in women. This was one of the aspects of *Émile* that women found most offensive, and Mary Wollstonecraft had raised similar angry objections to his promotion of deviousness and insincerity. The underlying theme of Edgeworth's work is her insistence that women are rational creatures in the same way as men, and if they act illogically or are swayed by their emotions, this does not illustrate a 'natural' flaw but is entirely a result of their inadequate education. Indeed, the whole point of education is to develop 'the reasoning faculty'.

The problem with the format Edgeworth chose for her work was that by putting her defence of women's education in the mouth of a father who was keen to reassure his friend that this would not lead women to seek to usurp male privileges, she was unable to display any of the indignant rhetoric that had made Mary Wollstonecraft's *Vindication of the Rights of Woman* so powerful. In 1798 she brought out a new edition and substantially rewrote the second letter, adding further examples to strengthen her argument and make it more lively. It is from this second edition that the following extract is taken.

❖

Maria Edgeworth
Letters for Literary Ladies
London: J. Johnson, 1798 (2nd edn)

Letter from a Gentleman to his Friend, Upon the Birth of a Daughter

I congratulate you, my dear sir, upon the birth of your daughter; and I wish that some of the fairies of ancient times were at hand to endow the damsel with health, wealth, wit and beauty. Wit? — I should make a long pause before I accepted of this gift for a daughter — you would make none.

As I know it to be your opinion that it is in the power of education, more certainly than it was ever believed to be in the power of fairies, to bestow all mental gifts; and as I have heard you say that education should begin as early as possible, I am in haste to offer you my sentiments, lest my advice should come too late.

Your general ideas of the habits and virtues essential to the perfection of the female character nearly agree with mine; but we differ materially as to the cultivation which it is necessary or expedient to bestow upon the understandings of women. You are a champion for the rights of woman, and insist upon the equality of the sexes; but since the days of chivalry are past, and since modern gallantry permits men to speak, at least to one another, in less sublime language of the fair; I may confess to you that I see neither in experience nor analogy much reason to believe that, in the human species alone, there are no marks of inferiority in the female — curious and admirable exceptions there may be, but many such have not fallen within my observation. I cannot say that I have been much enraptured, either on a first view or on a closer inspection, with female prodigies. Prodigies are scarcely less offensive to my taste than monsters; humanity makes us refrain from expressing disgust at the awkward shame of the one, whilst the intemperate vanity of the other justly provokes ridicule and indignation. I have always observed in the understandings of women who have been too much cultivated, some disproportion between the different faculties of their minds. One power of the mind undoubtedly may be cultivated at the expense of the rest, as we see that one muscle or limb may acquire excessive strength and an unnatural size, at the expense of the health of the whole body: I cannot think this desirable, either for the individual or for society. The unfortunate people in certain mountains of Switzerland are, some of them, proud of the excrescence by which they are deformed. I have seen women vain of exhibiting mental deformities which to me appeared no less disgusting. In the course of my life it has never been my good fortune to meet with a female whose mind, in strength, just proportion and activity, I could compare to that of a sensible man.

Allowing, however, that women are equal to our sex in natural abilities; from their situation in society, from their domestic duties, their taste for dissipation, their love of romance, poetry and all the lighter parts of literature, their time must be so fully occupied that they could never have leisure for, even supposing that they were capable of, that severe application to which our sex submit. Between persons of equal genius and equal industry, time becomes the only measure of their acquirements. Now calculate the time which is wasted by the fair sex, and tell me how much the start of us they ought to have in the beginning of the race, if they are to reach the goal before us? It is not possible that women should ever be our equals in knowledge, unless you assert that they are far our superiors in natural capacity. Not only time but opportunity must be wanting to complete female studies: we mix with the world without restraint, we converse freely with all classes of people, with men of wit, of science, of learning, with the artist, the mechanic, the labourer; every scene of life is open to our view; every assistance that foreign or domestic ingenuity can invent, to encourage literary studies, is ours almost exclusively. From academies, colleges, public libraries, private associations of literary men, women are excluded, if not by law, at least by custom, which cannot easily be conquered.

Whenever women appear, even when we seem to admit them as our equals in understanding, everything assumes a different form; our politeness, delicacy, habits towards the sex, forbid us to argue or to converse with them as we do with one another. We see things as they are; but women must always see things through a veil, or cease to be women. With these insuperable difficulties in their education and in their passage through life, it seems impossible that their minds should ever acquire that vigour and *efficiency* which accurate knowledge and various experience of life and manners can bestow.

Much attention has lately been paid to the education of the female sex; and you will say that we have been amply repaid for our care, that ladies have lately exhibited such brilliant proofs of genius as must dazzle and confound their critics. I do not ask for proofs of genius, I ask for solid proofs of utility. In which of the useful arts, in which of the exact sciences, have we been assisted by female sagacity or penetration? I should be glad to see a list of discoveries, of inventions, or observations, evincing patient research, of truths established upon actual experiment, or deduced by just reasoning from previous principles. If these or any of these can be presented by a female champion for her sex, I shall be the first to clear the way for her to the temple of Fame.

I must not speak of my contemporaries, else candour might oblige me to allow that there are some few instances of great talents applied to useful purposes; but except these, what have been the literary productions of women? In poetry, plays and romances, in the art of imposing upon the understanding by means of the imagination, they have excelled; but to useful literature they have scarcely turned their thoughts. I have never heard of any female proficients in science — few have pretended to science till within these few years. [...]

We are told, that as women are reasonable creatures, they should be governed only by reason; and that we *disgrace* ourselves, and *enslave* them, when we instil even the most useful truths as prejudices. Morality should, we are told, be founded upon demonstration, not upon sentiment; and we should not require human beings to submit to any laws or customs, without convincing their understandings of the universal utility of these political conventions. When are we to expect this conviction? We cannot expect it from childhood, scarcely from youth; but from the maturity of the understanding we are told that we may expect it with certainty. And of what use can it then be to us? When the habits are fixed, when the character is decided, when the manners are formed, what can be done by the bare conviction of the understanding? What could we expect from that woman, whose moral education was to begin, at the moment when she was called upon to *act*; and who, without having imbibed in her early years any of the salutary prejudices of her sex, or without having been educated in the amiable acquiescence to well established maxims of female prudence, should boldly venture to conduct herself by the immediate conviction of her understanding? [...]

Women of literature are much more numerous of late than they were a few years ago. They make a class in society, they fill the public eye, and have acquired a degree of consequence and an appropriate character. The esteem of private friends, and the admiration of the public for their talents, are circumstances highly flattering to their vanity; and as such I will allow them to be substantial pleasures. I am also ready to acknowledge that a taste for literature adds much to the happiness of life, and that women may enjoy to a certain degree this happiness as well as men. But with literary women this silent happiness seems at best but a subordinate consideration; it is not by the treasures they possess, but by those which they have an opportunity of displaying, that they estimate their wealth. To obtain public applause, they are betrayed too often into a miserable ostentation of their learning. Coxe tells us, that certain Russian ladies split their pearls, in order to make a greater display of finery.[4]

The pleasure of being admired for wit or erudition, I cannot exactly measure in a female mind; but state it to be as delightful as you can imagine it to be, there are evils attendant upon it which, in the estimation of a prudent father, may overbalance the good. The intoxicating effect of wit upon the brain has been well remarked by a poet who was a friend to the fair sex; and too many ridiculous and too many disgusting examples confirm the truth of the observation. The deference that is paid to genius sometimes makes the fair sex forget that genius will be respected only when united with discretion. Those who have acquired fame fancy that they can afford to sacrifice reputation. I will suppose, however, that their heads shall be strong enough to bear inebriating admiration; and that their conduct shall be essentially irreproachable, yet they will show in their manners and conversation that contempt of inferior minds, and that neglect of common forms and customs, which will provoke the indignation of fools, and which cannot escape the censure of the wise. Even whilst we are secure of their innocence, we dislike that daring spirit in the female sex which delighted to oppose the common opinions of society, and from apparent trifles we draw unfavourable omens, which experience too often confirms.

You will ask me why I should suppose that wits are more liable to be spoiled by admiration than beauties, who have usually a larger share of it,

---

[4] William Coxe (1748–1828), *Travels into Poland, Russia, Sweden and Denmark* (Dublin: S. Price et al., 1784).

and who are not more exempt from vanity? Those who are vain of trifling accomplishments, of rank, of riches or of beauty, depend upon the world for their immediate gratification. They are sensible of their dependence; they listen with deference to the maxims, and attend with anxiety to the opinions of those from whom they expect their reward and their daily amusements. In their subjection consists their safety; whilst women who neither feel dependent for amusement nor for self-approbation upon company and public places, are apt to consider this subjection as humiliating, if not insupportable. Perceiving their own superiority, they despise and even set at defiance the opinions of their acquaintance of inferior abilities; contempt, where it cannot be openly retorted, produces aversion, not the less to be dreaded because constrained to silence; envy, considered as the involuntary tribute extorted by merit, is flattering to pride; and I know that many women delight to excite envy, even whilst they affect to fear its consequences — but they who imprudently provoke it are little aware of the torments they prepare for themselves.

Answer to the Preceding Letter

[...] I will go farther, and at once give up to you all the learned ladies that exist, or have ever existed; but when I use the term literary ladies, I mean women who have cultivated their understandings not for the purposes of parade, but with the desire to make themselves useful and agreeable. I estimate the value of a woman's abilities and acquirements, by the degree in which they contribute to her happiness. You think yourself happy because you are wise, said a philosopher to a pedant. — I think myself wise because I am happy.

You tell me, that even supposing I could educate my daughter so as to raise her above the common faults and follies of her sex; even supposing I could give her an enlarged understanding, and literature free from pedantry, she would be in danger of becoming unhappy, because she would not, amongst her own sex, find friends suited to her taste, nor amongst ours, admirers adequate to her expectations: you represent her as in the situation of the poor flying-fish, exposed to dangerous enemies in her own element, yet certain, if she tries to soar above them, of being pounced upon by the hawk-eyed critics of the higher regions.

You allow, however, that women of literature are much more numerous of late than they were a few years ago; that they make a class in society, and have acquired a considerable degree of consequence, and an appropriate character; how can you then fear that a woman of cultivated understanding should be driven from the society of her own sex in search of dangerous companions amongst ours? In the female world she will be neither without an equal nor without a judge; she will not have much to fear from envy, because its malignant eye will not fix upon one object exclusively, when there are numbers to distract its attention, and share the stroke. The fragile nature of female friendships, the petty jealousies which break out at the ball or in the drawing-room, have been from time immemorial the jest of mankind. Trifles, light as air, will necessarily excite not only the jealousy, but the envy of those who think only of trifles. Give them more employment for their thoughts, give them a nobler spirit of emulation, and we shall hear no more of these paltry feuds; give them more useful and more interesting subjects of conversation, and they become not only more agreeable, but safe companions for each other. [...]

Even if literature were of no other use to the fair sex than to supply them with employment, I should think the time dedicated to the cultivation of their minds well bestowed: they are surely better occupied when they are reading or writing than when coqueting or gaming,[5] losing their fortunes or their characters. You despise the writings of women: you think that they might have made a better use of the pen, than to write plays, and poetry, and romances. Considering that the pen was to women a new instrument, I think they have made at least as good a use of it as learned men did of the needle some centuries ago, when they set themselves to determine how many spirits could stand upon its point, and were ready to tear one another to pieces in the discussion of this sublime question.[6] Let the sexes mutually forgive each other their follies; or, what is much better, let them combine their talents for their general advantage. You say, that the experiments we have made do not encourage us to proceed — that the increased care and pains which have been of late years bestowed upon female education have produced no adequate returns; but you in the same breath allow that amongst your contemporaries, whom you prudently forbear to mention, there are some instances of great talents applies to useful purposes. Did you expect that the fruits of good cultivation should appear before the seed was sown? You triumphantly enumerate the disadvantages to which women, from the laws and customs of society, are liable: they cannot converse freely with men of wit, science, and learning, nor even with the artist, or artificers; they are excluded from academies, public libraries, &c. Even our politeness prevents us, you say, from ever speaking plain truth and sense to the fair sex: every assistance that foreign or domestic ingenuity can invent to encourage literary studies, is, as you boast, almost exclusively ours: and after pointing out all these causes for the inferiority of women in knowledge, you ask for a list of the inventions and discoveries of those who, by your own statement of the question, have not been allowed opportunities for observation. With the insulting injustice of an Egyptian task-master, you demand the work, and deny the necessary materials.[7]

[5] That is, flirting or gambling at cards.
[6] The medieval Scholastic philosophers were derided for wasting their time on metaphysical debates such as the number of angels who could balance on the point of a pin or a needle.
[7] In Exodus ch. 5, the Egyptians demand that the enslaved Israelites should make bricks

[...]

Do not, my dear sir, call me a champion for the rights of woman;[8] I am too much their friend to be their partisan, and I am more anxious for their happiness than intent upon a metaphysical discussion of their rights: their happiness is so nearly connected with ours, that it seems to me absurd to manage any argument so as to set the two sexes at variance by vain contention for superiority. It ought not to be our object to make an invidious division of privileges, or an ostentations declaration of rights, but to determine what is most for our general advantage.

You fear that the minds of women should be enlarged and cultivated, lest their power in society and their liberty should consequently increase. Observe that the world *liberty*, applied to the female sex, conveys alarming ideas to our minds, because we do not stay to define the term; we have a confused notion that it implies want of reserve, want of delicacy; boldness of manners, or of conduct; in short, liberty to do wrong. — Surely this is a species of liberty which knowledge can never make desirable. [...]

It is, however, remarkable, that the means by which the sex have hitherto obtained that species of power which they have abused, have arisen chiefly from their personal, and not from their mental qualifications; from their skill in the arts of persuasion, and from their accomplishments; not from their superior powers of reason, or from the cultivation of their understanding. The most refined species of coquetry can undoubtedly be practised in the highest perfection by women, who to personal graces unite all the fascination of wit and eloquence. There is infinite danger in permitting such women to obtain power without having acquired habits of reasoning. Rousseau admires these sirens; but the system of Rousseau, pursued to its fullest extent, would overturn the world, would make every woman a Cleopatra, and every man an Antony; it would destroy all domestic virtue, all domestic happiness, all the pleasures of truth and love.

---

without straw. Since straw was a key ingredient, they were deliberately put in a position where the product would be found inadequate and they could be punished for it.

[8] A clear reference to Mary Wollstonecraft's *A Vindication of the Rights of Woman*.

— 10 —
Thomas Gisborne

Thomas Gisborne (1758–1846) was another member of the line of clerics who penned books of advice for women. He was writing thirty years after Fordyce and ten years after Bennett, and however dismissive their comments about women may now appear, they were mild when compared with Gisborne's repressive views. Whereas Fordyce was a society cleric preaching to fashionable congregations, Gisborne was an Evangelical clergyman writing after the horrors of the French Revolution, when many conservative commentators interpreted any move to alter society's norms in the direction of French-style 'liberty' as bound to result in destruction and bloodshed. Gisborne sternly preached that the role of women was not to be pleasing, as his earlier clerical colleagues had suggested, but to carry out their religious duty.

Gisborne was a friend of William Wilberforce and Hannah More, and a firm opponent of the slave trade. He was the rector of Barton in Staffordshire and a prebend of Durham Cathedral, and published a dozen religious and moral works throughout his long life. His *Enquiry into the Duties of the Female Sex*[1] was first published in 1797 and runs to nearly 450 pages, full of crushingly long sentences and multiple subordinate clauses. It nevertheless proved very popular, and by 1823 had reached its thirteenth London edition, but it does not appear to have been reprinted in Dublin or in the United States.

Gisborne first defines the distinctive characteristics of the female mind, and then prescribes an education fitted to it. He held the conventional view that women's minds are different from men's, and regarded women's incapacity for sustained analytical thought as the deliberate intention of God, who gives his creatures the skills they will need for their allotted station in life. Women will not need bodily strength or mental acuity since their lives will be restricted to the domestic sphere, and it would be a waste to award them such capacities. He espoused the standard belief that women are inferior in intellect but superior in feelings of the heart: 'modesty, delicacy, sympathising sensibility, prompt and active benevolence, warmth and tenderness of attachment'. Like Fordyce and Bennett, he admits there are a few exceptions, but they are of no consequence

---

[1] Thomas Gisborne, *Enquiry into the Duties of the Female Sex* (London: T. Cadell & W. Davies, 1797).

and do not invalidate his rule.

He does not of course expect, or even intend, to make women more like men. They may aspire to be perfect in their own way, but male virtues are inappropriate to them. The object of women's education should be to counteract the errors and temptations which derive from the peculiarities of the female character, causing their unsteadiness of mind, fondness of novelty, habits of frivolousness, dislike of sober application, vanity and affectation, caprice, and irritability. It is women's lauded superior imagination that makes them liable to sudden excesses, suspicion, fretfulness and groundless discontent. The chief aim of education should be 'to engage the understanding and the affections of the pupil in favour of piety and virtue, and to detach the mind from that supreme love of worldly objects to which it is prone'.

He is pleased to note that teaching has recently improved, and now aims to enrich girls' minds with knowledge, but with the caveat that this must be suitable to their sex. This includes the 'ornamental' accomplishments (dancing, drawing, French, Italian), but a girl should be taught that these are not for public display but merely to fill her long hours of solitude while her husband is away carrying out his important duties. Geography and history may be taught, selected aspects of natural history (nothing immodest, we may assume), and popular and amusing scientific facts.

He recommends that a woman should spend part of each day reading improving books that 'may contribute to her virtue, her usefulness, and her innocent satisfaction, to her happiness in this world and in the next'. Once she has read the Bible and religious works, she may turn to history, biography or poetry, but her studies must be confined 'within the strictest limits of purity'. Novels and romances are banned, of course, since most of them are improper to be 'perused by the eye of delicacy'.

Gisborne is aware that young women sometimes complain that they have nothing to do and can look forward only to a life of 'dismal vacuity', but he regards this as completely without foundation. There are many acceptable ways in which they can keep busy: helping their mothers in the house, visiting the sick and aged, helping the female poor of the neighbourhood, and supporting hospitals for women and schools for children. Such philanthropic activities are not only consistent with their natural sympathy for others but are also 'in the precise line of female duty'.

He then turns to the question of marriage and matrimonial life, and is firm in condemning any derogation from the prescribed relationship of domination and submission. This is a matter not even open to discussion, for it is ordained by God:

> Whether marriage establishes between the husband and the wife a perfect equality of rights, or conveys to the former a certain degree of superiority

over the latter, is a point not left among Christians to be decided by speculative arguments. The intimation of the divine will, communicated to the first woman immediately after the fall, is corroborated by various injunctions delivered in the New Testament.[2]

God has wisely assigned pre-eminence to the husband, since he has the burden of those offices in life which require 'the greatest exertions, the deepest reflection, and the most comprehensive judgement' and he has accordingly 'been furnished by his Creator with powers of investigation and of foresight in a somewhat larger measure than the other sex, who have been recompensed by an ample share of mental endowments of a different kind'.

And woe betide the wife who thinks she can exercise these mental endowments to suggest she knows better than her husband: even if she is aware of her influence over him, she must never display it or dare to 'intrude into those departments which belong not to her jurisdiction'. She must be 'content with the province which reason and revelation have assigned to her, and sedulous to fulfil, with cheerful alacrity, the duties which they prescribe'. She has obtained her husband's regard by her 'artless attractions' and must beware lest she lose it through 'unwarrantable and teasing competition'. If she has any learning, she must conceal it, for men will not tolerate even 'the most distant appearance of rivalship' in any woman, least of all a wife.

As far as we know, Gisborne had never been to France or attended one of the salons hosted by Parisian ladies. He made no reference in his work to Rousseau, the impious foreigner, but nevertheless closely mirrored Rousseau's attack on the salons as the archetype of female impertinence.

> If, conformably to the example heretofore exhibited in polite life at Paris, a real or supposed eminence in intellectual endowments were generally to inflame a lady with a propensity to erect herself into an idol for the votaries of science and taste to worship: were it to fill her with ambition to give audience to a levee of deistical philosophers; to see her toilet surrounded with wits and witlings; to pronounce to the listening circle her decision on a manuscript sonnet; and to appreciate the versification and the point of the last new epigram which aspired to divert the town; it would neither have been denied nor regretted that a female so qualified would, in this country, be deemed one of the least eligible of wives.[3]

Fortunately for the gentlemen of Britain, the number of ladies of this description

---

[2] Gisborne, *Enquiry*, pp. 226–27. This refers to the punishment of Eve in Genesis 3. 16, when she was told by God that 'thy desire shall be to thy husband, and he will rule over thee', and also to St Paul's admonition in Ephesians 5. 22–24, 'Wives, submit yourselves to your own husbands as unto the Lord. For the husband is the head of the wife as Christ is the head of the church [...] Therefore as the church is subject unto Christ, so let the wives be to their own husbands in everything' (King James Version).

[3] Gisborne, *Enquiry*, pp. 265–66.

'does not appear likely to swell to such an excess, as to alarm the other sex with the prospect of greatly narrowing the circle from which partners for the connubial state are to be selected'. The method of education he recommends is of course designed to prevent the emergence of learned ladies and to increase the pool of acceptable wifely material.

Gisborne's exhortations may not have been universally heeded in his own family. His daughter Lydia, married to a Yorkshire clergyman, became the object of the passions of her children's young tutor, Branwell Brontë, and they may have been lovers. After nearly three years in her household he was abruptly dismissed and returned home in a state of depression and self-pity. Branwell's literary sisters were of course to write novels expressing women's frustrated ambitions, whilst hiding their identity behind assumed masculine names.

❖

Thomas Gisborne
An Enquiry into the Duties of the Female Sex
London: A. Strahan, 1801 (5th edn)

Chapter III. On the Peculiar Features by which the Character of the Female Mind is Naturally Discriminated from that of the Other Sex

It would perhaps be no unfair representation of the sentiment which prevailed in the last age, to affirm that she who was completely versed in the sciences of pickling and preserving, and in the mysteries of cross-stitch and embroidery; she who was thoroughly mistress of the family receipt-book[4] and of her needle, was deemed, in point of solid attainments, to have reached the measure of female perfection. Since that period, however, it has been universally acknowledged, that the intellectual powers of women are not restricted to the arts of the housekeeper and the sempstress.[5] Genius, taste, and learning itself, have appeared in the number of female endowments and acquisitions. And we have heard, from time to time, some bold assertors of the rights of the weaker sex stigmatizing, in terms of indignant complaint, the monopolising injustice of the other; laying claim, on behalf of their clients, to co-ordinate authority in every department of science and of erudition; and upholding the perfect equality of injured woman and usurping man in language so little guarded, as scarcely to permit the latter to consider the labours of the camp and of the senate as exclusively pertaining to himself.[6]

The Power who called the human race into being has, with infinite wisdom,

---

[4] 'Receipt' means recipe.
[5] 'Sempstress' means seamstress or needlewoman.
[6] The camp and the senate stand for military and political careers, both regarded as off-limits to women.

regarded, in the structure of the corporeal frame, the tasks which the different sexes were respectively destined to fulfil. To man, on whom the culture of the soil, the erection of dwellings, and, in general, those operations of industry, and those measures of defence, which include difficult and dangerous exertion, were ultimately to devolve, He has imparted the strength of limb, and the robustness of constitution, requisite for the persevering endurance of toil. The female form, not commonly doomed, in countries where the progress of civilisation is far advanced, to labours more severe than the offices of domestic life, He has cast in a smaller mould, and bound together by a looser texture. But to protect weakness from the oppression of domineering superiority, those whom He has not qualified to contend, He has enabled to fascinate; and has amply compensated the defect of muscular vigour by symmetry and expression, by elegance and grace. To me it appears, that He has adopted, and that He has adopted with the most conspicuous wisdom, a corresponding plan of discrimination between the mental powers and disposition of the two sexes.

The science of legislation, of jurisprudence, of political economy; the conduct of government in all its executive functions; the abstruse researches of erudition; the inexhaustible depths of philosophy; the acquirements subordinate to navigation; the knowledge indispensable in the wide field of commercial enterprise; the arts of defence, and of attack, by land and by sea, which the violence or the fraud of unprincipled assailants render needful; these, and other studies, pursuits, and occupations, assigned chiefly or entirely to men, demand the efforts of a mind endued with the powers of close and comprehensive reasoning, and of intense and continued application, in a degree in which they are not requisite for the discharge of the customary offices of female duty.

It would therefore seem natural to expect, and experience, I think, confirms the justice of the expectation, that the Giver of all good, after bestowing those powers on men with a liberality proportioned to the subsisting necessity, would impart them to the female mind with a more sparing hand. It was equally natural to expect, that in the dispensation of other qualities and talents, useful and important to both sexes, but particularly suited to the sphere in which women were intended to move, He would confer the larger portion of his bounty on those who needed it the most. It is accordingly manifest, that, in sprightliness and vivacity, in quickness of perception, in fertility of invention, in powers adapted to unbend the brow of the learned, to refresh the over-laboured faculties of the wise, and to diffuse throughout the family circle the enlivening and endearing smile of cheerfulness, the superiority of the female mind is unrivalled.

Chapter IV. On Female Education

The primary end of education is to train up the pupil in the knowledge, love, and application of those principles of conduct, which, under the superintending influence of the divine mercy, will lead probably to a considerable share of happiness in the present life, but assuredly to a full measure of it in that which is to come. The secondary end is, to superadd to the possession of right principles those improving and ornamental acquisitions, which, either from their own nature, or from the prevailing customs of a particular age and country, are in some degree material to the comfort and to the usefulness of the individual. The difference in point of importance which subsists between these two objects is such, that the dictates of sober judgement are palpably abandoned, whenever the latter is suffered, in the slightest manner, to encroach on the priority of the former. The modes of attaining both objects, and of pursuing the second in due subordination to the first, require to be adjusted according to the circumstances which characterise the persons who are to receive instruction. Hence in female education, that instructor is ignorant or regardless of a duty of the highest concern, who, in transfusing into the youthful hearer those fundamental truths which equally concern every human being, does not anxiously point out their bearings on the particular weaknesses and errors, whether in judgement or in action, into which the female sex is in especial danger of being betrayed. An attempt to efface the discriminating features, which the hand of God has impressed on the mind, is in every case impossible to accomplish: and would be in every case, were it practicable, the height of folly and presumption. To efface those of the female mind, would be to deprive women of their distinguishing excellences. [...]

In the cultivation of the female understanding essential improvements have taken place in the present age. Both in schools and in private families there prevails a desire to call forth the reasoning powers of girls into action, and to enrich the mind with useful and interesting knowledge suitable to their sex. The foundation is laid by communicating to the scholar a rational insight into the formation and idioms of her native tongue. The grammatical blunders, which used to disgrace the conversation even of women in the upper and middle ranks of life, and in conjunction with erroneous orthography to deform their epistolary correspondence,[7] are already so much diminished, that in some years hence it may perhaps no longer be easy to find a young lady, who professes to be mistress of the French language, and is at the same time grossly ignorant of her own. Geography, select parts of natural history, and of the history of different nations, ancient or modern, popular and amusing facts in astronomy and in other sciences, are often familiar to the daughter in a degree which, at

---

[7] Women's spelling was notoriously erratic.

the very moment that it delights the parent, reminds her how small a portion of such information was in her youth imparted to herself.

Of the books, also, which have been published within the last twenty years for the purpose of conveying instruction to girls, though some of them approach too nearly to the style and sentiments of romances, a considerable number possesses great merit; and most of them are abundantly more adapted to interest the young reader, and thus to make a lively and permanent impression on her understanding, than those were which they have succeeded. [...]

To impart to the youthful scholar those acquisitions which are desired either considerably or entirely on the score of ornament, constitutes, as was stated in the outset, the second branch of Education. That this branch of education is not at present undervalued or neglected in our own country, is a fact, which even a slight knowledge of the general proceedings and opinions of parents in the upper and middle classes of society would be sufficient to establish beyond the probability of dispute. Two questions remain to be proposed. First, whether it is valued and cultivated too much? Secondly, whether the prevailing modes of cultivating it are judicious: that is to say, whether it is kept subordinate, and sufficiently subordinate, to the primary object of instruction, the inculcation of those radical principles on which present and future happiness depends;[8] and whether, in the manner as well as in the degree of carrying it on, due regard is paid to the peculiar characteristics of the female mind, and to the impressions, the errors, and the dangers to which, in consequence of those native peculiarities, the scholar is exposed? The answer which must be given to these questions, an answer to be deduced from general practice, not from a few scattered exceptions, is not the reply which it were highly to be wished that truth would have permitted to be returned. In schools, almost universally, and very commonly, I fear, in domestic tuition, ornamental accomplishments occupy the rank and estimation which ought to have been assigned to objects of infinitely greater importance. [...]

Is it surprising that a young woman should give free scope to the desires, which she has ever been led to cherish; that she should practise the arts, in which her childhood was initiated? Is it surprising that she, when grown up, should starve herself into shapeliness, and overspread her face with paint, who was trained at a boarding-school to swing daily by the chin, in order to lengthen her neck, and perhaps even accustomed, as is sometimes the case, to peculiar modes of discipline contrived to heighten the complexion. If she was taught throughout the whole course of her education, though not by express precept, yet by daily and hourly admonitions which could convey no other meaning, that dancing is for display, that music is for display, that drawing and French and Italian are for display; can it be a matter of astonishment, that during

---

[8] By 'radical' he means fundamental.

the rest of her life she should be incessantly on the watch to shine and to be admired? [...]

Let the pupil, then, be thoroughly impressed with a conviction of the real end and use of all such attainments; namely, that they are designed, in the first place, to supply her hours of leisure with innocent and amusing occupations; occupations which may prevent the languor and the snares of idleness, render home attractive, refresh the wearied faculties, and contribute to preserve the mind in a state of placid cheerfulness, which is the most favourable to sentiments of benevolence to mankind and of gratitude to God: and in the next place, to enable her to communicate a kindred pleasure, with all its beneficial effects, to her family and friends, to all with whom she is now, or may hereafter be, intimately connected.

– 11 –
Priscilla Wakefield

Priscilla Wakefield (1751–1832) was a writer of popular children's books on botany, entomology and travel. She came from a Quaker family, married a London merchant and had three children of her own. She started writing in her forties to support her family through financial difficulties, and her books were designed to teach useful facts in a way that was easy for children to understand. She was a strong supporter of the anti-slavery movement, and lived to the age of eighty-one.

Wakefield was also a successful practical philanthropist. She founded a lying-in hospital for women and a school for girls, who were taught reading and writing as well as needlework and arithmetic. The venture which had the longest-lasting effect was a Penny Savings Bank she founded in Tottenham to help those on low wages to save money; this became enormously popular with labourers and servants, both men and women, and the idea spread throughout the country.

We should bear in mind this practical experience and concern about social welfare when reading Wakefield's views on women's education. Though clearly a devout woman, she did not promote religion as the unique solution to society's problems or enjoin the poor to suffer their lot with due humility (though she was no political radical). She recognised the general expectation that women would be supported throughout their lives by their fathers or husbands, but was troubled by the fate of those who found themselves unable to rely on male support and ended up destitute, with no means of earning a living other than prostitution. Her principal message was that women should be educated in such practical occupations as would enable them to earn an independent income, should this be necessary. Knowledge would not be sufficient: social attitudes would have to change to make this acceptable, and appropriate professions opened to them.

In 1798 she published a book entitled *Reflections on the Present Condition of the Female Sex: with Suggestions for its Improvement*.[1] This was brought out by Joseph Johnson, the radical publisher who was frequently responsible for

---

[1] Priscilla Wakefield, *Reflections on the Present Condition of the Female Sex: with Suggestions for its Improvement* (London: J. Johnson, 1798).

putting before the public works by religious dissenters. The book opens with a quotation from Adam Smith, whose *Wealth of Nations* had first appeared twenty years earlier, to the effect that any individual who does not contribute his share of productive labour is a burden on society. Wakefield did not wish to argue about the relative talents of men and women, but only to point out that the current state of education for women was inadequate for them to develop their natural abilities.

Wakefield was aware that women who had dared to 'stray beyond the accustomed path' had often been condemned both by men and by other women, and that people feared that too much learning might tempt them into immorality, but she reassured her readers that there were types of learning and useful occupations that were consistent with female modesty and decorum. Unfortunately, the only ambition most families had for their daughters was that they should make an advantageous marriage, and everything they were taught was part of the 'science of pleasing'.

Wakefield's recommendation — a highly original one for her time — was that day-schools should be established for the four different classes of society. She defined these as first the nobility or those in high office; secondly the learned professions, landowners and wealthy merchants or manufacturers; thirdly farmers, tradesman and artisans; and finally the labouring poor.

It was the first two classes that found the idea of a woman working for her living unacceptable, but Wakefield pointed out that anyone can lose her relatives to untimely death, and the recent French wars had filled the streets with widows and orphans who would not have fallen into degradation had they been trained in some skill that would have enabled them to support themselves.

Wakefield did not believe that the virtues of men and women were different, and asserted that if a man is praised for working to support himself and his family, so should a woman be. She expressed astonishment that in England, where a man could be engaged in commerce and still be considered respectable, a woman who did so would be banished from polite society, and young men regarded it as demeaning to marry a girl 'who has been trained up to any profitable employment'. She confronted one of the main fears lying behind this prejudice, that educated women would become too assertive, and observed that the prejudice against women's education arose from men's fear that 'by teaching women too much, and by rendering them too useful, they should become independent of them'.

The rest of the book consists of a proposed course of study for each of the four classes, designed to fit their social function. Upper-class women will not only run their households, educate their children and supervise their servants, but also take on the role of inspecting poorhouses (which had a high infant death rate), and take an interest in girls in charity schools. Their curriculum includes languages, simple mathematics, astronomy, history, and natural and experimental science.

The second class of women need to learn economy and the art of managing expenditure. They should be taught cookery, basic accounting and simple medicine, and learn childcare by looking after the smaller children in the family. These women should also practice benevolence, by taking the lead in the promotion and supervision of charitable institutions. They should take an interest in the welfare of their servants and encourage them to improve themselves, and teach the poor budgeting, cleanliness and self-organisation. To prepare them for these activities, such girls should be taught a more limited number of subjects in greater depth, including English grammar, literature, history, biography and poetry. They will also learn simple mathematics and book-keeping. Their amusements will be books and conversation, which cost little.

The subject so far has been girls whose destiny will be to manage or supervise their husband's households. But what should be done for those who have no male support and have fallen into poverty, but 'whose refinement of manners unfit them for any occupation of a sordid menial kind'? Wakefield recommends that their occupations must be 'neither laborious nor servile' but struggles to find many acceptable choices. She suggests 'pursuits which require the exercise of intellectual, rather than bodily powers', which will not require them to leave the home, and gives as an example fine arts such as painting. She admits that not many women have excelled at painting, but is sure this is because few have tried it. There are lesser aspects of the arts that they could aspire to, such as designs and sketches for books, needlework patterns, miniature painting, watercolours of animals and plants for books of natural history, colouring maps, or designs for fabrics and wallpaper.

The third class of women are the daughters of tradesmen, who will have to work alongside their fathers or husbands. To prepare them for their future they should learn reading, spelling, writing, arithmetic, geometry and practical needlework. No plays or novels are included, of course, for these will lead them to the allurements of vice.

Wakefield was troubled by the limited opportunities for such women to find paid employment, and their unjust treatment when they did. Unusually for her time, she was concerned about inequality of wages, observing that it was unfair that a footman was paid much more than a kitchen-maid. Many occupations that had traditionally been filled by women had been taken over by men, who were then paid more; these included hairdressers, dress-makers and even corset-makers, and Wakefield pleads that wealthy women should help by patronising women in these trades. She also insists that only women should serve in shops which sell articles for female consumption; this should apply particularly to haberdashers, perfumers, milliners, and shops selling gloves and shoes. Undertakers should employ women to lay out the female dead, and male teachers should be replaced by women in girls' schools.

A woman without the protection of a man was particularly vulnerable, and Wakefield refers obliquely to girls being raped by their apprentice-master or his sons, or by idle lackeys. She wishes to encourage marriage and the formation of stable relationships among the lower classes but notes the practical obstacles in their way: domestic servants are forced to leave their jobs if they marry, so their employers should help them to save some of their earnings, or give them a monetary gift when they leave service, so they can set up in some other business. She makes a direct link between the prevalence of prostitution and women's difficulty in finding employment, and is firm in her view that women are driven to prostitution not through moral laxity but because they are seduced and abandoned by men. They have no other way to live.

The lowest class of women should also receive a school education appropriate to their station. They are to be given simple instruction in the doctrines of Christianity and short lessons on morality, enough reading and writing to be able to calculate their expenditure, and otherwise will learn washing, ironing, knitting and mending linen, indeed 'every other qualification that will prepare them to become useful as servants, or as the wives of labourers'. In these schools beatings will not be allowed.

Priscilla Wakefield showed a practical attitude to improving the prospects of impoverished women by teaching them to earn their living. Her book was reprinted in 1817, and some of her ideas were adopted by individual charitable projects such as her own girls' school in Tottenham, but it was to be some time before they were absorbed into a systematic approach to national education. Her family continued her patient work of social improvement: her niece was Elizabeth Fry, the celebrated campaigner for the reform of women's prisons.

❖

Priscilla Wakefield
Reflections on the Present Condition of the Female Sex:
with Suggestions for its Improvement
London: J. Johnson, 1798

It is asserted by Doctor Adam Smith that every individual is a burthen upon the society to which he belongs, who does not contribute his share of productive labour for the good of the whole. The doctor, when he lays down this principle, speaks in general terms of man as a being capable of forming a social compact for mutual defence and the advantage of the community at large. He does not absolutely specify that both sexes, in order to render themselves beneficial members of society, are equally required to comply with these terms; but since the female sex is included in the idea of the species, and as women possess the same qualities as men, though perhaps in a different degree, their sex cannot free them from the claim of the public for their proportion of usefulness. That the major part of the sex, especially of those among the higher orders, neglect to fulfil this important obligation, is a fact that must be admitted, and points out the propriety of an enquiry into the causes of their deficiency.

The indolent indulgence and trifling pursuits in which those who are distinguished by the appellation of gentlewomen often pass their lives, may be attributed with greater probability to a contracted education, custom, false pride and idolizing adulation, than to any defect in their intellectual capacities. The contest for equality in the mental capacity of the sexes has been maintained on each side of the question with ingenuity; but as a judgment only can be formed from facts, as they arise in the present state of things, if the experiments have been fairly tried, the rare instances of extraordinary talents which have been brought forward to support the system of equality must yield to the irresistible influence of corporeal powers. Which leads to a conclusion that the intellectual faculties of each sex are wisely adapted to their appropriate purposes, and that, laying aside the invidious terms of superiority and inferiority, the perfection of mind in man and in woman, consists in a power to maintain the distinguishing characteristics of excellence in each. But this concession by no means proves, that even in this enlightened age and country, the talents of women have ever been generally exerted to the utmost extent of their capacity, or that they have been turned towards the most useful objects; neither does it imply that the cultivation they receive is adequate to bring into action the full strength of those powers, which have been bestowed on them by nature. The intellectual faculties of the female mind have too long been confined by narrow and ill-directed modes of education, and thus have been concealed, not only from others, but from themselves, the energies of which they are capable.

The exigence of circumstances in private life has called for the numberless examples of female prudence, magnanimity and fortitude,[2] which demonstrated no less a clearness of conception than a warmth of feeling, reflecting equal honour upon the heads and upon the hearts of the sex. Neither has history been silent in recording memorable instances of female capacity in all the various branches of human excellence.

These united testimonies are surely sufficient to justify an opinion that the imperfect contributions to the mass of public activity have not arisen from a want of ability to be useful, but from some defect of another kind, which it is necessary to discover, that a remedy may be found and applied to the evil.

---

[2] Prudence, magnanimity and fortitude had long been regarded as exclusively masculine virtues.

In civilized nations it has ever been the misfortune of the sex to be too highly elevated, or too deeply depressed: now raised above the condition of mortals, upon the score of their personal attractions, and now debased below that of reasonable creatures, with respect to their intellectual endowments. The result of this improper treatment has been a neglect of the mental powers, which women really possess but know not how to exercise; and they have been contented to barter the dignity of reason for the imaginary privilege of an empire, of the existence of which they can entertain no reasonable hope beyond the duration of youth and beauty.

Of the few who have raised themselves to pre-eminence by daring to stray beyond the accustomed path, the envy of their own sex, and the jealousy or contempt of the other, have too often been the attendants; a fate which doubtless has deterred others from attempting to follow them or emulate, even in an inferior degree, the distinction they have attained.

But notwithstanding these disadvantages, and others of less perceptible influence, the diffusion of Christianity and the progress of civilization have raised the importance of the female character; and it has become a branch of philosophy not a little interesting, to ascertain the offices which the different ranks of women are required to fulfil. Their rights and their duties have lately occupied the pens of writers of eminence; the employments which may properly exercise their faculties, and fill up their time in a useful manner, without encroaching upon those professions which are appropriate to the men, remain to be defined.

There are many branches of science, as well as useful occupations, in which women may employ their time and their talents, beneficially to themselves and to the community, without destroying the peculiar characteristic of their sex, or exceeding the most exact limits of modesty and decorum. Whatever obliges them to mix in the public haunts of men, or places the young in too familiar a situation with the other sex; whatever is obnoxious to the delicacy and reserve of the female character, or destructive in the smallest degree to the strictest moral purity, is inadmissible. The sphere of feminine action is contracted by numberless difficulties that are no impediments to masculine exertion. Domestic privacy is the only sure asylum for the juvenile part of the sex; nor can the grave matron step far beyond that boundary with propriety. Unfitted by their relative situation in society for many honourable and lucrative employments, those only are suitable for them which can be pursued without endangering their virtue or corrupting their manners.

But under these restrictions there may be found a multitude of objects adapted to the useful exertions of female talents, which it will be the principal design of these Reflections to point out, after making some remarks upon the present state of female education, and suggesting some improvements towards its reformation.

And here the author may perhaps be allowed to express her hope that among the numbers of the female world who appear to be satisfied with inferiority, many require only to be awakened to a true sense of their own real consequence, to be induced to support it by a rational improvement of those hours which they have hitherto wasted in the most frivolous occupations. The promotion of so useful a design is the only apology for intruding her opinions upon the subject; and it will be esteemed her highest recompense, should her observations contribute to its accomplishment.

— 12 —
Mary Hays

Mary Hays (1759–1843) was a friend of Mary Wollstonecraft, and was both admired and vilified as her closest disciple. When Wollstonecraft died in 1797, Hays wrote a fulsome obituary, mentioning her 'masculine tone of understanding', as well as her more conventionally feminine humanity and sensibility.[1] She praised her 'ardent, ingenuous, unconquerable spirit', and her 'exertions to awaken in the minds of her oppressed sex a sense of their degradation, and to restore them to the dignity of reason and virtue'.

Mary Hays was born into a large family in Southwark, on the banks of the Thames in London. She fell in love with a young man who lived nearby, but he died two weeks before the date of their wedding. She saw this as the end of her hopes for the traditional female roles of marriage and motherhood, and described it as the defining moment of her life.

Hays learned from a young age not to be afraid to challenge social orthodoxy. Like Wakefield and Wollstonecraft, she was a member of one of the Dissenting sects: these devout Christians who did not conform to the doctrines and practices of the established Church of England were often political and social nonconformists as well. Since they were excluded from the universities, they established their own educational institutions, many of which became admired for their quality and rigour. However, these were open only to men, and Mary attributed her own education to the influence of Robert Robinson (1735–1790), a Baptist preacher who corresponded with her and provided her with books, and insisted on 'the right of private judgment'. Robinson educated his daughters as well as his sons in languages, mathematics and natural sciences, and this encouraged Hays in her pursuit of knowledge.

She joined the circle at the New College in Hackney that included such proponents of liberty as the Rev. Richard Price and the scientist Joseph Priestley. Following the French Revolution, and in particular when Britain went to war with France in 1793, all these men became politically suspect. In that year, Hays published her first book, *Letters and Essays, Moral and Miscellaneous*, which attempted to explain radical Enlightenment ideas to a female audience, and entered the argument about the need to educate women

---

[1] *Monthly Magazine*, IV, September 1797, pp. 232–33.

so that they might choose virtue after rational consideration, with a tribute to Mary Wollstonecraft:

> I cannot mention the admirable advocate for the rights of women [...] without pausing to pay a tribute of grateful respect in the name of my sex, I will say, of grateful respect, to the virtue and talents of a writer, who with equal courage and ability hath endeavoured to rescue the female mind from those prejudices by which it has been systematically weakened, and which have been the canker of genuine virtue; for purity of heart can only be the result of knowledge and reflection.[2]

She followed this in 1796 with a novel, *The Memoirs of Emma Courtney*, a semi-autobiographical work whose heroine, a reader of Rousseau's *Émile* and *Julie*, writes a series of intimate letters to a man who fails to reciprocate her passion. The book had mixed reviews, with some readers feeling uncomfortable with Emma's explicit expressions of desire for her unresponsive lover.

Hays' second novel, published in 1799, was even more shocking to public opinion. The heroine of *The Victim of Prejudice* is the bastard daughter of a prostitute, and herself becomes the victim of rape. The novel portrays these events as the fault of society and its institutions, and not of the women themselves. The Tory *Anti-Jacobin Review* advised her contemptuously to give up writing and return to her distaff, the traditional emblem of female domesticity,[3] and described her as having the soul of a prostitute without the physical attractions to match.[4]

In 1798 Hays published anonymously *An Appeal to the Men of Great Britain in Behalf of Women*.[5] She explained in the preface that she had written the work some years before, but had been discouraged from publishing it after reading Wollstonecraft's *Rights of Woman* and discovering that all her points had already been made. She had nevertheless decided that it might be beneficial to make the case in a less challenging way: a genius like Wollstonecraft, who has no patience with the prejudices of mankind, might find it difficult 'to make new and unexpected truths palatable to common minds', whereas Hays will endeavour to persuade her readers to accept a 'gradual reformation' and 'gentle emancipation from error'.[6]

Despite this disclaimer, the work is a hard-hitting polemic. It talks about men as domestic tyrants who subject women to cruel injustice. She claims that men deliberately restrict women's education, for fear that they might learn about their rights and refuse to play the submissive role that men demand. She points

---

[2] Mary Hays, *Letters & Essays Moral & Miscellaneous* (London: T. Knott, 1793), p. vi.
[3] *Anti-Jacobin Review*, 1799, III, p. 58.
[4] *Anti-Jacobin Review*, January 1800, p. 94.
[5] Mary Hays, *An Appeal to the Men of Great Britain in Behalf of Women* (London: J. Johnson, 1798).
[6] *Appeal*, Advertisement to the Reader (unpaginated).

out the hypocrisy of men who demand that women transform themselves into domestic wives and mothers while seeing no need to improve their own immoral behaviour, and she proclaims that the thing men fear most is 'the frightful certainty of having women declared their equals'.

The *Appeal* was noted briefly by the *Monthly Magazine*, and given a longer treatment in the *Analytical Review*,[7] published by the radical printer Joseph Johnson; this set out Hays' arguments in cogent form, though with a tone that suggested the reviewer found them exaggerated. The reviewer concluded by mockingly praising his country's political leadership for resisting every possible move for reform on the grounds that permitting 'the dominion of truth and reason' would 'strike at the root of wealth'.

In 1803, Hays published a six-volume compendium of famous historical women entitled *Female Biography*;[8] this comprised potted histories of nearly three hundred women, including queens, artists, poets, dramatists and translators, dating from Classical times until her own day. Seven years earlier, she had claimed that 'the rights of women and the name of Wollstonecraft, will go down to posterity with reverence',[9] but following the outcry when Wollstonecraft's husband William Godwin published his *Memoirs* and exposed her unconventional lifestyle,[10] Hays felt it prudent to omit her friend from the list of illustrious women, though she did have the courage to include Catharine Macaulay, who was by then almost equally unpopular.

Mary Hays continued to write and publish until 1817, but rapidly fell out of the public eye. By the time of her death in 1843 at the age of eighty-four, Queen Victoria was on the throne, but no other woman in Britain dared to claim a role in public life.

Note on the Text

The text seems to have been printed as soon as it was written, without review or revision. It is prolix and repetitive and includes a number of evident errors. I have amended the punctuation, which is full of random commas and dashes and in its original form is very distracting.

---

[7] *Monthly Magazine*, 6 December 1798, p. 520; Analytical *Review* (28 July 1798), pp. 23–36.
[8] Mary Hays, *Female Biography: Memoirs of Illustrious & Celebrated Women of All Ages & Countries* (London: Richard Phillips, 1803).
[9] Mary Hays, *Letters & Essays*, p. 21.
[10] William Godwin, *Memoirs of the Author of A Vindication of the Rights of Woman* (London: J. Johnson, 1798).

Mary Hays
An Appeal to the Men of Great Britain in Behalf of Women
London: J. Johnson, 1798

We have now considered the characters of women, as men would have them to be, and as they really are; though I must confess in that slight, hasty, and unfinished manner, of which in some degree every part of this little work must necessarily partake. By the arrangement of my subject I should next proceed to WHAT WOMEN OUGHT TO BE; but before I take upon me to delineate that very important part of it, I shall make some reflections which may serve to connect what I have already advanced, with that which I have still further to say on the subject.

I have heretofore, it is true, been pretty free in my observations upon the conduct of men, where I think it absurd and capricious with regard to women; but I hope without acrimony, for I am sure I feel none towards them. On the contrary I love them with all my heart as individuals. But even themselves must own that taken collectively, they are inclined to be a little too consequential, a little too tyrannical, a little too desirous of assuming an exclusive right to all power, wisdom, knowledge, and learning.

In justice however to men, let us now enquire why in general they are so averse from women acquiring knowledge of almost any sort? And why with regard to those attainments in particular which enlarge the understanding and strengthen the judgment, they say, 'Thus far shalt thou go, and no further'?

I think then it must be the opinion of every sensible and impartial person, man and woman, who takes the trouble to consider the subject coolly, that it is from no bad motive — that indeed it can be from no bad motive, if we reflect how inseparably their own happiness is connected with that of women's [*sic*] — that men have in almost all nations, and in all ages, nearly agreed in this system of intellectual privation with regard to the other sex. But I fear we must add that they act upon a bad principle, or perhaps we should rather say upon a wrong one.

Let me here explain myself clearly.

While then we wish to exonerate[11] men with respect to the motives which prompt their conduct towards women, while we cannot upon any fair principles of reasoning doubt that they are desirous, and even satisfied, that good consequences may follow from their absolute government of women; we cannot with any degree of sincerity profess that we consider as well established, but on the contrary as false — or at best but as uncertain — that principle upon which

---

[11] The text says 'exhonor'.

they build their whole system, viz. THAT MEN ARE SUPERIOR BEINGS, WHEN COMPARED WITH WOMEN; AND THAT CONSEQUENTLY NATURE AND REASON INVEST THEM WITH AUTHORITY OVER THE WEAKER SEX. This, divested of all ambiguity of language, and all attempts to impose on the understandings or compound with the vanity of women, is beyond a doubt not the opinion only of the generality of men, but the leading principle upon which the laws by which we are governed are founded, the grand pivot upon which social and domestic politics turn — and the language of prejudice all over the world. For, alas for poor human nature, it yet remains to be proven that it is the language of truth. What is it indeed after all but an opinion taken up at random, and which perhaps if fairly examined and cross examined, may be found to be the essence, nay the very quintessence, of prepossession, of arrogance and of absurdity!

But it must be confessed that even those who consider the human species in a more liberal and extensive point of view, who do not see sufficient grounds for those claims so haughtily advanced on the part of the men, yet suppose the necessity of subordination on one side unavoidable. They therefore fear that women, were their eyes opened to their natural equality and consequence, would not so tamely submit to the cruel injustice with which they are treated in many of the leading points in life. And they know that nothing would tend so much to this *éclaircissement* as an education, which by exercising their reason and unfolding their talents, should point out to themselves how they might exert them to the utmost. Such a development of mind would undoubtedly enable them to see and reason upon what principles all the other regulations of society were formed, which, however they may deviate in execution, are evidently founded on justice and humanity; and would consequently enable them to bring home and apply those principles to the situation of their sex in general. Thus awakened to a sense of their injuries, they would behold with astonishment and indignation the arts which had been employed to keep them in a state of PERPETUAL BABYISM.

I know that many will be inclined to think that to keep millions of reasonable beings in ignorance of their own rights, merely that they may not have it in their power to claim them, is doing a bad thing from the worst of motives. But let us consider further, that men not only fear that if women were permitted to be what they call too wise, and knowing, they would not so easily submit to be governed; but they likewise fear that this want of submission, might produce the most fatal consequences in society. [...]

Notwithstanding then that men have planned every thing their own way, I must repeat that the consequences are not equal to their hopes or expectations; for they complain bitterly both in public and private, of the folly, the inconsistency, the extravagance, and the general relaxation of manners amongst women. And they would be extremely well satisfied if, without changing an iota of their own system and self indulgence, they could transform women in general into domestic wives, tender mothers, and dutiful and affectionate daughters; characters upon which they expatiate with enthusiasm and delight, and no wonder. But when it is at any time argued and proved that to bring about reformation, the first step ought to be the reformation of the moral conduct of the men themselves; and the next that of educating women on a more liberal and unprejudiced plan, and putting them on a more respectable footing in society; then it is that the generality of men fly off, and are not ashamed to declare that they would rather a thousand times take women as they are — weak frail, dependent creatures. In comparison of the frightful certainty of having women declared their equals, and as such their companions and friends, instead of their amusement, their dependents, and in plain and unvarnished terms their slaves, folly, vice, impertinence of every kind is delightful. [...]

And here a question naturally occurs which is sometimes disputed, but generally negatived. Whether women should receive nearly the same education as men, with exceptions which are obvious to common sense, and which the delicacy of the female frame, and the still greater delicacy of the female character, prove to be undeniably founded in nature? Even after these exceptions are granted, I allow that the question has been generally negatived. But by whom, and who were the judges? Why men to be sure, and men only; for the party most deeply concerned are [sic] never consulted, but considered, upon I know not what principle, as totally incompetent to judge. [...]

When men, however, deign to argue more to the point, they allege that when women are educated too much upon an equality with them, it renders them presuming and conceited; useless[12] in their families; masculine, and consequently disgusting in their manners.

These are very heavy charges indeed, but women do not allow them to be well founded, nor unanswerable.

The first objection advanced is that knowledge and learning render women presuming and conceited. I beg leave to say that both reason and experience contradict this assertion; for it has never been proven that knowledge in a general view favoured or produced presumption, though in particular instances it may no doubt be found to have done so. Much it must be confessed depends on the subject acted upon, and knowledge may be compared with respect to its effects on the mind to wholesome food upon the body; for a diseased habit will turn the purest aliments to corruption instead of nourishment. But this only confirms what has been so often and so well said, that there is no rule without exception.

Thus I will not pretend to deny but that some women who have a great deal of knowledge are neither so amiable, nor so useful members of society, as

---

[12] The text says 'unless'.

others who have little or none, above what is necessary in the most common occurrences in life. But does not this likewise apply to men of the same description? And what does it after all prove? Nothing but that the most valuable acquisitions may in particular instances be perverted and misapplied. If this, however, were allowed to be a sufficient objection, we scarcely know anything which could stand so severe a test. For all sublunary good is liable to be perverted to evil. We may then be permitted to say that upon the whole, knowledge has a direct and natural tendency to promote the love and the consequent practice of virtue, to improve the mind, to exercise and strengthen the judgment, and to correct the heart. In short, under the guidance of reason and religion, to conduct mankind to every possible perfection. At least if this is not acknowledged, we can give no good reason why men should adopt the acquisition of it as necessary and ornamental to themselves.

Since then this doctrine will not, nor indeed cannot be denied with regard to men, reasoning from analogy, I do not conceive that it can be denied when applied to women. For even allowing what cannot be very easily proven, that there is a difference in degree, they are closely, so very closely akin, that whatever applies to the one does to the other, with very slight deviations.

Indeed knowledge, learning and all solid acquirements are as yet so very rare among the female sex that it is by no means surprising if some who really possess those advantages know it and feel it. Nor is it surprising, nor perhaps altogether out of nature, though by no means commendable or pleasing, if they at times endeavour to let others know it and feel it too. Yet to the honor of both sexes be it said — to the honor of human nature and learning be it spoke — instances of proud and presumptuous persons of real abilities and solid acquirements are but rare, in comparison of the numbers who are the delight of their friends, the ornaments of society and the benefactors of mankind. It were possible to enumerate names well known to the world and dear to their own circle, who are equally admired in an amiable as in a literary point of view. Suffice it to say that the experience of the present times as well as of past ages fully justify [sic] us in maintaining that, a few exceptions granted which prove nothing, knowledge does improve everyone, man or woman, who is blessed with common sense for a foundation; that presumption and conceit are rather the offspring of ignorance than knowledge; and that knowledge of almost any description is better than ignorance. Always without a doubt, however, preferring that kind most suited to situation and circumstances, and which, as far as human foresight can judge, is most likely to be useful and ornamental through life.

The charge which we shall next endeavour to prove erroneous is that the pursuit and possession of knowledge occasion in women a neglect of their families and domestic duties. Perhaps this is the charge of all others the worst founded, the consequence the least likely to happen were we to trust to theory, and the most decidedly contradicted when we appeal to facts and experience. Surely knowledge, learning and science give a solidity to the mind, a turn for reflection, which must be highly favorable to the best feelings of humanity, and consequently to the most amiable of all the affections, the parental. Not that I mean to say that women are wanting in this virtue who have no pretensions to those; though to say the truth, the parental fondness of many mothers often more resembles animal instinct, blind partiality and personal vanity, than that rational affection which leads to the improvement as well as to the preservation of the human species. And when added to that ignorance of the powers of the mind to which most part of the female sex are condemned, we take into consideration the flimsy, inconsequent education generally bestowed upon them, we cannot be surprised if instead of training, it unfits them for the important task — the serious attention — requisite to form the minds as well as to care for the bodies of their children. [...]

While then on the one hand we see that women who are not educated with some degree of attention to mental and useful attainments are too much occupied with fashionable gaieties or other frivolous amusements to make domestic virtues and duties their concern; and while it is evident that their habits and pursuits are at eternal variance with these; it will hardly be denied upon the other hand, that the habits and pursuits of women of reading and reflection are highly favorable, and assimilate, if I may so express myself, with every home enjoyment and social delight. Home indeed is to them the scene of their happiness, their refuge from noise and folly, the center of their wishes, to which all their desires and actions ultimately tend; the magnet whose attraction counterbalances that of the world, and keeps them in a steady and uniform course. Not shunning with fastidious nicety nor ill-founded scruples the innocent pleasures and elegant amusements of the times; but ever considering these as the relaxations only, not as the serious business of life. And being well convinced that true happiness, like true virtue, shuns all extremes, they will endeavour to attain it by that mixture of home joys and social intercourse with the world; which, as most congenial to human nature, is not only most conducive to present enjoyment but to future and progressive improvement.

The reader may think I have drawn these two characters — that of a mere woman of the world and that of a woman of an improved understanding — with a partial hand. It is impossible perhaps that any reasonable person contemplating both should do otherwise. Yet with all due allowance for this, the portraits are drawn from nature, and consequently consistent with truth. For as to exceptions, they affect not any system.

Having said as much on the two first charges as the limited nature of this sketch will admit, I shall now consider the last — that knowledge renders women masculine, and consequently disgusting in their manners. In doing this, I think my argument will prove a two-edged sword. I think it must prove that neither has learning a direct and inevitable tendency to render women masculine, nor if it did so, would it render them consequently and infallibly disagreeable to the men.

Perhaps to define the terms used is one of the first duties of writers; and if they always understood themselves, and made their readers clearly comprehend the precise meaning of them, much labored reasoning and many false and presumptuous conclusions might be spared. For example, when we speak of a masculine woman, it is considered as a term of reproach, yet we do not consider whether it deserved to be so or not. We allow ourselves to be run away with by a vague idea, an undefined term, of which we do not take the trouble to know the precise meaning or the exact bounds.

If therefore we are to understand by a masculine woman one who emulates those virtues and accomplishments which, as common to human nature, are common to both sexes, the attempt is natural, amiable and highly honourable to that woman, under whatever name her conduct may be disguised or censured. For even virtue and truth may be misnamed, disguised and censured, but they cannot change their natures in compliance with the tyranny of fashion and prejudice. These may indeed for a time throw a shade over them, but this once removed, we find them still the same — IMMUTABLE and ETERNAL. It is in vain perhaps, therefore, honestly speaking and impartially, to attempt to make any very serious distinctions between the virtues and accomplishments of the sexes. We may indeed dress out these somewhat differently, to suit a reigning taste or through love of variety, and we may call this manners, by which if women can please the other sex without materially injuring themselves, they ought most certainly to do so. But such vain distinctions vanish before the superior light of reason and religion, and women in all the different stations in life find scope for the exercise of every virtue of which human nature is capable. And under the passive characters of humility, resignation and absolute submission to their authority — under these do men expect to see exercised and exerted everything which they in their proud moments arrogate to themselves, and fondly claim as sole proprietors.

— 13 —
Hannah More

The conventional sentiments expressed in the works of Hannah More (1745–1833) were belied by the story of her life; she insisted that women should restrict themselves to domestic duties, whilst herself benefiting from public renown, agitating against the slave trade, engaging in practical philanthropy, and writing strongly-worded letters to bishops and politicians. Her collected works ran to nineteen volumes, and during her lifetime she outsold Jane Austen many times over. She also reaped the financial rewards, leaving the considerable sum of £30,000 in her will.[1]

Hannah was born in Bristol in 1745 and lived to be nearly ninety years old. She was the fourth of five daughters of a schoolmaster who gave them a broad education, but stopped Hannah's lessons when she showed too much mathematical ability: reading Latin literature was acceptable, since it might enable women to learn morally uplifting sentiments, but mathematics was too abstract an intellectual exercise for a woman, and might result in that dangerous creature: a female pedant.

She was keen on writing from an early age, and when only seventeen published a moral and sentimental play in verse that went on to sell an astounding 10,000 copies. In 1773 she set off for London, where she had the good fortune to make the acquaintance of David Garrick, the celebrity actor-manager; Garrick encouraged Hannah to write plays, and arranged for some of them to be performed. Hannah soon became part of London's literary scene; she associated with Samuel Johnson and Edmund Burke, and attended Elizabeth Montagu's Bluestocking salon, where she met Hester Chapone and Catharine Macaulay.

Hannah's plays were less well-received after Garrick's death, and in the early 1780s she experienced a religious conversion, following which her life took a much more serious turn. She abandoned her London society friends and moved to Somerset, where she lived with her sister Martha for all but the last five years of her life. Through her friendship with Beilby Porteus, the Bishop of London, she came to know Wilberforce and other members of the evangelical Clapham Sect, and became a prominent opponent of the slave trade.

---

[1] Equivalent to over £3 million today.

In 1789 Hannah visited the nearby village of Cheddar, and was appalled by the wretched state of the agricultural workers there. She was equally shocked to discover that the rector of Cheddar had not visited the parish for years, leaving the population to suffer in soul as well as body. Hannah and her sisters decided to set up schools for the poor, but ran into strong resistance from the landowners, who saw nothing but harm in educating the poor above their station, and from the clergy, who accused her of Methodism. She got round this by establishing Sunday Schools, since this was the one day when the workers were entitled to a day off, and over the course of the next ten years set up eleven schools in the locality, where she and her sisters taught reading, writing and arithmetic, and gave lessons in the Bible and the catechism. Three of these schools were to survive into the twentieth century.

The 1790s saw considerable social unrest in Britain, with riots in major cities and demands for increased political rights. The government countered with occasional brutality, and in 1795 banned seditious meetings. It was feared that the English lower orders were being infected with radical and atheistic ideas imported from the Continent, and especially from France.

More was called upon to exercise her literary talents in this cause, and between 1792 and 1797 wrote many simple moral tales, designed to inspire their readers to individual moral virtues (hard work, abstinence from alcohol) and contentment with the current political structures. Her stories were original and entertaining, and written in accessible language. The first was *Village Politics*,[2] a dialogue between Jack the blacksmith and Tom the mason. Jack has been reading Thomas Paine, and decides he wants 'Liberty and Equality, and the Rights of Man', like the French. Tom mocks him for his naivety, pointing out that in Britain the law protects all classes and the constitution is infinitely superior to that in France. For three years More churned out these 'Cheap Repository Tracts', in which the righteous are always rewarded and the wicked punished, and the politically conservative prevail over radical thinkers. In one year alone, two million copies were published, making her one of the most widely-read authors in the country.

In 1799, More published *Strictures on the Modern System of Female Education*, beginning with the complaint that 'It is a singular injustice which is often exercised towards women, first to give them a most defective education, and then to expect from them the most undeviating purity of conduct'.[3]

As a devout Christian, she was particularly agitated by the fact that in contemporary high society, for a woman to display a fervent belief in religion

---

[2] *Village Politics: addressed to all the Mechanics, Journeymen and Day-Labourers in Great Britain, by Will Chip, a Country Carpenter* (York: G. Walker, 1792).
[3] Hannah More, *Strictures on the Modern System of Female Education*, 2 vols (London: T. Cadell & W. Davies, 1800), 8th edn, I, p. ix.

would be regarded as ridiculous. She condemned Rousseau's *Julie* which, by portraying as its heroine a woman who has taken a lover but is still admired as virtuous, 'strikes at the very root of honour, by elevating a crime into a principle'. She recognised the insidious attractions of his ideas, and of his prose: 'Perhaps there never was a net of such exquisite art, and inextricable workmanship, spread to entangle innocence and ensnare inexperience, as the writings of Rousseau'. More was herself an eloquent writer: her prose is full of vivid metaphors, and it is not surprising that she was so popular with the reading public.

More also opposed the view of reforming philosophers that the problems of society are caused by inadequate organisation and can be solved by political or social reform. In her view, the root of these problems is moral weakness, and must be met by a return to the eternal principles of religion. She was wholly a disciple of Burke in regarding the structure of society as reflecting an immutable divine plan, venerable in its antiquity, which we tamper with at our peril. In fact, she seemed to reject the whole Enlightenment project, and condemned all 'speculative philosophy' as fundamentally immoral.

It is clear that for her the aim of education is not to keep women busy, or to make them more interesting conversationalists, or even to train them to run their households efficiently, but to save their souls and reform their characters. The business of education is 'to implant right ideas, to communicate useful knowledge, to form a correct taste and a sound judgment, to resist evil propensities, and above all to seize the favourable season for infusing principles and confirming habits; if education be a school to fit us for life, and life be a school to fit us for eternity'.

More condemns the cult of sensibility, since by making emotion the touchstone of truth it enables each individual to choose his or her own morality and tends to 'reduce all mental and moral excellence into sympathy and feeling'. But while women should not act as helpless creatures, neither should they attempt to be more like men, for this will only result in 'the bold and independent beauty, the intrepid female, the hoyden' with 'swinging arms' and 'confident address' who, in trying not to please men but to rival them, will find herself overlooked by potential suitors.

Nor is she impressed by the time girls spend on acquiring 'accomplishments'. She sees no point in their learning French or Italian, since hardly any of them are ever likely to meet a foreigner. The teaching of music has gone so far as to be ridiculous: 'The science of music, which used to be communicated in so competent a degree to a young lady by one able instructor, is now distributed among a whole band. She now requires, not a master, but an orchestra'.

More shared the views of those who believed women to be incapable of equalling men in sustained analytical thought. However, she did suggest that these intellectual limitations might be due, at least in part, to the more circumscribed nature of their lives: 'till women shall be more reasonably educated, and till the native growth of their mind shall cease to be stinted and cramped, we have no [just] ground for pronouncing that their understanding has already reached its highest point'.

If women cannot lead the life of the intellect, should not waste their time on accomplishments, and have no part to play in public life, what then is left to them? Hannah's answer, which she put into practice in her own life, was philanthropy, driven by the principles of Christian charity. She was convinced that women did have an important role to play in society: to display and encourage a high seriousness that would reform manners and return people to religion, the only source of enduring morality.

More's admiring biographer, William Roberts, observed after her death that:

> Those females who are desirous of consulting Mrs More's moral works for the direction of their conduct, and they cannot consult a safer guide, or a better practical expounder of scriptural rules and injunctions, must bear to be told of domestic duties, and of the inexpediency and danger of deserting home, and its various appropriate and important offices, for the sake of playing a more conspicuous part in the field of diffusive benevolence.[4]

It must also be observed that she aimed to reinforce the hierarchical social structure, and make people — both men and women — content to spend their lives carrying out their duty in the station in which had God had placed them, with the confidence that they would receive their reward in the life to come. This helps to explain her outrage towards the end of her life when she perceived other people to be educating the poor beyond their station. In a letter to her friend Sir William Pepys she admitted that 'my views of popular instruction are narrow', and recalled how her own schools had taught only reading, writing and arithmetic, 'which was all I thought necessary for *labourers*' children'. She had been reading with horror a book by an 'ultra-educationist' which appeared to suggest 'that there is *nothing* which the poor ought not to be taught'. They were supposed to learn science and classical history, and even if they could afford to buy the necessary books, she could not see how they would find time to read them without neglecting their business and violating their duty. She tried to use her influence in high places to have this stopped: 'I have exerted my feeble voice to prevail on my few parliamentary friends to steer the middle way between the Scylla of brutal ignorance and the Charybdis of a literary education. The one is cruel, the other preposterous'.[5]

Two years later, she returned to the theme in a letter to William Wilberforce,

---

[4] *Memoirs of the Life & Correspondence of Mrs Hannah More*, ed. by Roberts, IV, p. 432.
[5] Letter to Sir William Weller Pepys, 1821, in *The Letters of Hannah More*, ed. by R. Brimley Johnson (London: Bodley Head, 1925), pp. 198–99.

protesting that 'not only in the great national schools, but in the little paltry cottage seminaries of three-pence a week, I hear of the most ridiculous instances of the affectation of *literature*'. She recounts inquiring of a servant girl what she was reading, and asking if she could recite her catechism. The child, to Hannah's evident disgust, replied 'Oh no, Madam, I am learning *Syntax*'.[6] She feared that the more education people — both men and women — received, the more rights they would demand. In this she was, of course, absolutely correct.

❖

Hannah More
Strictures on the Modern System of Female Education
London: T. Cadell & W. Davies, 1800, 8th edn[7]

The practical use of female knowledge, with a sketch of the female character, and a comparative view of the sexes.

The chief end to be proposed in cultivating the understandings of women is to qualify them for the practical purposes of life. Their knowledge is not often like the learning of men, to be reproduced in some literary composition, nor ever in any learned profession; but it is to come out in conduct. It is to be exhibited in life and manners. A lady studies, not that she may qualify herself to become an orator or a pleader; not that she may learn to debate, but to act. She is to read the best books, not so much to enable her to talk of them, as to bring the improvement which they furnish, to the rectification of her principles and the formation of her habits. The great uses of study are to enable her to regulate her own mind, and to be instrumental to the good of others.

To woman, therefore, whatever be her rank, I would recommend a predominance of those more sober studies, which, not having display for their object, may make her wise without vanity, happy without witnesses, and content without panegyrists; the exercise of which will not bring celebrity, but improve usefulness. She should pursue every kind of study which will teach her to elicit truth; which will lead her to be intent upon realities; will give precision to her ideas; will make an exact mind. She should cultivate every study which, instead of stimulating her sensibility, will chastise it; which will neither create an excessive or a false refinement; which will give her definite notions; will bring the imagination under dominion; will lead her to think, to compare, to combine, to methodise; which will confer such a power of discrimination that her judgment shall learn to reject what is dazzling, if it be not solid; and to prefer, not what is striking, or bright, or new, but what is just. That

---

[6] Letter to William Wilberforce, 1823, in *The Letters of Hannah More*, p. 202.
[7] The first edition was published in 1799. More revised the text for this later edition by adding words and phrases to make her argument even more forceful.

kind of knowledge which is rather fitted for home consumption than foreign exportation, is peculiarly adapted to women.

It is because the superficial mode of their education furnishes them with a false and low standard of intellectual excellence, that women have too often become ridiculous by the unfounded pretensions of literary vanity: for it is not the really learned, but the smatterers, who have generally brought their sex into discredit, by an absurd affectation, which has set them on despising the duties of ordinary life. There have not indeed been wanting (but the character is not now common) *precieuses ridicules*,[8] who, assuming a superiority to the sober cares which ought to occupy their sex, have claimed a lofty and supercilious exemption from the dull and plodding drudgeries *of this dim speck called earth*!

There have not been wanting ill-judging females, who have affected to establish an unnatural separation between talents and usefulness, instead of bearing in mind that talents are the great appointed instruments of usefulness; who have acted as if knowledge were to confer on woman a kind of fantastic sovereignty, which should exonerate her from the discharge of female duties; whereas it is only meant the more eminently to qualify her for the performance of them. A woman of real sense will never forget, that while the greater part of her proper duties are such as the most moderately gifted may fulfil with credit, (since Providence never makes that to be very difficult, which is generally necessary) yet that the most highly endowed are equally bound to perform them; and let her remember that the humblest of these offices, performed on Christian principles, are wholesome for the minds even of the most enlightened, and they tend to the casting down of those 'high imaginations' which women of genius are too much tempted to indulge.

For instance; ladies whose natural vanity has been aggravated by a false education, may look down on *economy*[9] as a vulgar attainment, unworthy of the attention of an highly cultivated intellect; but this is the false estimate of a shallow mind. Economy, such as a woman of fortune is called on to practise, is not merely the petty detail of small daily expenses, the shabby curtailments and stinted parsimony of a little mind, operating on little concerns; but it is the exercise of a sound judgment exerted in the comprehensive outline of order, of arrangement, of distribution; of regulations by which alone well governed societies, great and small, subsist. She who has the best regulated mind will, other things being equal, have the best regulated family. As in the superintendence of the universe, wisdom is seen in its *effects*; and as in the visible works of

---

[8] Molière's satirical play *Les Précieuses Ridicules* was first performed in Paris in 1659, and mocked the Parisian salon ladies who used affected vocabulary in order to appear ultra-refined, and pretended to a degree of learning they did not truly possess.

[9] The term 'economy' encompassed the management of an estate or household, which was often the wife's responsibility. It incorporated but was not limited to the sense of being 'economical' by saving on expenses.

Providence, that which goes on with such beautiful regularity is the result not of chance but of design; so that management which seems the most easy is commonly the consequence of the best concerted plan. A sound economy is a sound understanding brought into action; it is calculation realised; it is the doctrine of proportion reduced to practice; it is foreseeing consequences, and guarding against them; it is expecting contingencies and being prepared for them. The difference is that to a narrow minded vulgar economist the details are continually present; she is overwhelmed by their weight, and is perpetually bespeaking your pity for her labours, and your praise for her exertions: she is afraid you will not see how much she is harassed. She is not satisfied that the machine moves harmoniously, unless she is perpetually exposing every secret spring to observation. Little events, and trivial operations engross her whole soul; while a woman of sense, having provided for their probable recurrence, guards against the inconveniences, without being disconcerted by the casual obstructions which they offer to her general scheme. Subordinate expenses and inconsiderable retrenchments should not swallow up that attention which is better bestowed on regulating the general scale of expense, correcting and reducing an overgrown establishment, and reforming radical and growing excesses.

Superior talents however are not so common as, by their frequency, to offer much disturbance to the general course of human affairs; and many a lady who tacitly accuses herself of neglecting her ordinary duties because she is a *genius*, will perhaps be found often to accuse herself as unjustly as good St. Jerome, when he laments that he was beaten by the Angel for being too Ciceronian in his style.[10]

The truth is, women who are so puffed up with the conceit of talents as to neglect the plain duties of life, will not frequently be found to be women of the best abilities. And here may the author be allowed the gratification of observing, that those women of real genius and extensive knowledge, whose friendship have conferred honour and happiness on her own life, have been in general eminent for economy, and the practice of domestic virtues; and have risen superior to the poor affectation of neglecting the duties and despising the knowledge of common life, with which literary women have been frequently, and not always unjustly, accused. [...]

But there is one *human* consideration which would perhaps more effectually tend to damp in an aspiring woman the ardours of literary vanity (I speak not of real genius, though there the remark often applies) than any which she will derive from motives of humility, or propriety, or religion; which is, that in the judgment passed on her performances, she will have to encounter the

---

[10] St Jerome recorded a dream in which he was beaten by an angel for being too interested in Classical learning rather than scripture.

mortifying circumstance of having her sex always taken into account, and her highest exertions will probably be received with the qualified approbation, *that it is really extraordinary for a woman*. Men of learning, who are naturally apt to estimate works in proportion as they appear to be the result of art, study, and institution, are apt to consider even the happier performances of the other sex as the spontaneous productions of a fruitful but shallow soil; and to give them the same sort of praise which we bestow on certain salads, which often draw from us a sort of wondering commendation; not indeed as being worth much in themselves, but because by the lightness of the earth, and a happy knack of the gardener, these indifferent cresses spring up in a night, and therefore we are ready to wonder they are no worse. [...]

But *they* little understand the true interests of woman who would lift her from the duties of her allotted station, to fill with fantastic dignity a loftier but less appropriate niche. Nor do they understand her true happiness, who seek to annihilate distinctions from which she derives advantages, and to attempt innovations which would depreciate her real value. Each sex has its proper excellencies, which would be lost were they melted down into the common character by the fusion of the new philosophy. Why should we do away distinctions which increase the mutual benefits and satisfactions of life? Whence, but by carefully preserving the original marks of difference stamped by the hand of the Creator, would be derived the superior advantage of mixed society? Is either sex so abounding in perfection as to be independent of the other for improvement? Have men no need to have their rough angles filed off, and their harshnesses and asperities smoothed and polished by assimilating with beings of more softness and refinement? Are the ideas of women naturally so *very* judicious, are their principles so *invincibly* firm, are their views so *perfectly* correct, are their judgments so *completely* exact, that there is occasion for no additional weight, no superadded strength, no increased clearness, none of that enlargement of mind, none of that additional invigoration which may be derived from the aids of the stronger sex? What identity could advantageously supersede such an enlivening opposition? Is it not then more wise as well as more honourable to move contentedly in the plain path which Providence has obviously marked out to the sex, and in which custom has for the most part rationally confirmed them, rather than to stray awkwardly, unbecomingly, and unsuccessfully, in a forbidden road? Is it not desirable to be the lawful possessors of a lesser domestic territory, rather than the turbulent usurpers of a wider foreign empire? to be good originals, than bad imitators? to be the best thing of one's own kind, rather than an inferior thing even if it were of an higher kind? to be excellent women rather than indifferent men?

Is the author then undervaluing her own sex? — No. It is her zeal for their true *interests* which leads her to oppose their imaginary *rights*. It is her regard for their happiness which makes her endeavour to cure them of a feverish thirst for fame as unattainable as inappropriate; to guard them against an ambition as little becoming the delicacy of their female character as the meekness of their religious profession. A little Christian humility and sober-mindedness are worth all the empty renown which was ever obtained by the misapplied energies of the sex; it is worth all the wild metaphysical discussion which has ever been obtruded under the name of reason and philosophy; which has unsettled the peace of vain women, and forfeited the respect of reasonable men. And the most elaborate definition of ideal rights, and the most hardy measures for attaining them, are of less value in the eyes of a truly amiable woman, than 'that meek and quiet spirit, which is in the sight of God of great price.'

Natural propensities best mark the designations of Providence as to their application. The fin was not more clearly bestowed on the fish that he should swim, nor the wing given to the bird that he should fly, than superior strength of body and a firmer texture of mind was given to man, that he might preside in the deep and daring scenes of action and of council; in the complicated arts of government, in the contention of arms, in the intricacies and depths of science, in the bustle of commerce, and in those professions which demand a higher reach, and a wider range of powers. The true value of woman is not diminished by the imputation of inferiority in those talents which do not belong to her, of those qualities in which her claim to excellence does not consist. She has other requisites, better adapted to answer the end and purposes of her being, from 'HIM who does all things well'; who suits the agent to the action; who accommodates the instrument to the work.

Let not then aspiring, because ill-judging woman, view with pining envy the keen satirist, hunting vice through all the doublings and windings of the heart; the sagacious politician leading senates, and directing the fate of empires; the acute lawyer detecting the obliquities of fraud; and the skilful dramatist, exposing the pretensions of folly; but let her ambition be consoled by reflecting, that those who thus excel, to all that Nature bestows and books can teach, must add besides that consummate knowledge of the world to which a delicate woman has no fair avenues, and which even if she could she attain she would never be supposed to have come honestly by.

In almost all that comes under the description of polite letters, in all that captivates by imagery, or warms by just and affecting sentiment, women are excellent. They possess in a high degree that delicacy and quickness of perception, and that nice discernment between the beautiful and defective, which comes under the denomination of taste. Both in composition and action they excel in details; but they do not so much generalize their ideas as men, nor do their minds seize a great subject with so large a grasp. They are acute observers, and accurate judges of life and manners, as far as their own sphere of observation extends; but they describe a smaller circle. A woman sees the world, as it were, from a little elevation in her own garden, whence she takes an exact survey of home scenes, but takes not in that wider range of distant prospects, which he who stands on a loftier eminence commands. Women have a certain tact which often enables them to feel what is just more instantaneously than they can define it. They have an intuitive penetration into character, bestowed on them by Providence, like the sensitive and tender organs of some timid animals, as a kind of natural guard, to warn of the approach of danger beings who are often called to act defensively.

In summing up the evidence, if I may so speak, of the different powers of the sexes, one may venture, perhaps, to assert, that women have equal *parts*, but are inferior in *wholeness* of mind, in the integral understanding: that though a superior woman may possess single faculties in equal perfection, yet there is commonly a juster proportion in the mind of a superior man: that if women have in an equal degree the faculty of fancy which creates images, and the faculty of memory which collects and stores ideas, they seem not to possess in equal measure the faculty of comparing, combining, analysing, and separating these ideas; that deep and patient thinking which goes to the bottom of a subject; nor that power of arrangement which knows how to link a thousand connected ideas in one dependent train, without losing sight of the original idea out of which the rest grow, and on which they all hang. The female too, wanting steadiness in her intellectual pursuits is turned aside by her characteristic tastes and feelings. Woman in the career of genius, is the Atalanta, who will risk losing the race by running out of her road to pick up the golden apple;[11] while her male competitor, without, perhaps, possessing greater natural strength or swiftness, will more certainly attain his object, by being less exposed to the seductions of extraneous beauty, and will win the race, not by excelling in speed, but by despising the bait.[12]

Here it may be justly enough retorted, that, as it is allowed the education of women is so defective, the alleged inferiority of their minds may be accounted for on that ground more justly than by ascribing it to their natural make. And, indeed, there is so much truth in the remark, that till women shall be more reasonably educated, and till the native growth of their mind shall cease to be stinted and cramped, we have no juster ground for pronouncing that their understanding has already reached its highest attainable point, than the

---

[11] In the ancient myth, Atalanta could outrun any man, but her suitor Hippomenes was given three golden apples by the goddess Aphrodite which he threw in her path to distract her, and thus won the race.

[12] Author's footnote: What indisposes even reasonable women to concede in these points is, that the weakest man instantly lays hold on the concession; and, on the mere ground of sex, plumes himself on his own individual superiority; inferring that the silliest man is superior to the first rate woman.

Chinese would have for affirming that their women have attained to the greatest possible perfection in walking, while the first care is, during their infancy, to cripple their feet.[13] At least, till the female sex are more carefully instructed, this question will always remain as undecided as to the *degree* of difference between the masculine and feminine understanding, as the question between the understandings of blacks and whites; for until men and women, and until Africans and Europeans are put more nearly on a par in the cultivation of their minds, the shades of distinction, whatever they may be, between their native abilities can never be fairly ascertained.[14] [...]

And let the weaker sex take comfort, that in their very exemptions from privileges which they are sometimes disposed to envy, consist not only their security but their happiness. If they enjoy not the distinctions of public life and dignified offices, do they not escape the responsibility attached to them, and the mortification of being dismissed from them? If they have no voice in deliberative assemblies, do they not avoid the load of duty inseparably attached to such privileges? Preposterous pains have been taken to excite in women an uneasy jealousy, that their talents are neither rewarded with public honours nor emoluments in life; nor with inscriptions, statues, or mausoleums after death. It has been absurdly represented to them as a hardship, that while they are expected to perform duties, they must yet be contented to relinquish honours, and must unjustly be compelled to renounce fame while they must labour to deserve it.

---

[13] The Chinese custom of foot-binding for women was known to Europeans, who regarded it with horror.

[14] The 1799 edition here adds: 'Thus, though in what relates to the actual difference of mind in the sexes, the distinction itself seems clearly marked by the defining finger of the Creator, yet of the *degree* of that native difference a just estimate can never be formed till the understandings of women are made the most of; till, by suffering their intellectual powers to take the lead of the sensitive in their education, their minds shall be allowed to reach to that measure of perfection of which they are really susceptible, and which their Maker intended they should attain.'

CONCLUSION

It might appear from the texts in this collection that by the end of the eighteenth century Rousseau's views on the nature and function of women had prevailed, and the few flashes of resistance around the time of the French Revolution had been defeated by a reaction so firm that the concept of educating women for anything beyond a strictly domestic role had vanished for ever. We know, of course, that this did not happen.

It would be wrong to mistake prescription for description: behind the commanding tones of a Fordyce or a Gisborne we may sometimes detect a hint of desperation, as they looked around them at groups of giggling girls or contemplated the latest female-authored novel. If all women were behaving in the way they thought appropriate, they would have had no need to condemn them in such harsh tones or to spend so many pages explaining to them their duties and obligations.

The ensuing Victorian age did indeed adopt the concept of woman as the 'angel in the house' as its social ideal, but this ignored not only the lived reality of the millions of women who had no choice but to work — in shop, factory and field — but also the frustrations of middle-class girls who longed for the opportunities offered to their brothers.

The concept of rights that took physical form in the French Revolution did not die, despite reaction and repression: Hannah More lived to see the 1832 Reform Act, which enfranchised millions of working men and, only a week before her death in September 1833, the abolition of slavery that she had longed for. And less than twenty years later, Frances Buss set up North London Collegiate School with the deliberate aim of offering girls the same educational opportunities as boys, and Bedford College was established as the first institute of higher education for women in Britain. This was shortly followed by the pioneering Elmira College in the United States, and in New York in 1849 Elizabeth Blackwell became the first woman to qualify as a doctor.

We may be sure that Jean-Jacques Rousseau would not have approved.

BIBLIOGRAPHY

Modern Critical Editions of Original Texts in English

EDGEWORTH, MARIA, ED. BY CLAIRE CONNOLLY, *Letters for Literary Ladies* (London: Everyman Library, J. M. Dent, 1993)

GENLIS, STÉPHANIE-FÉLICITÉ DE, ED. BY GILLIAN DOW, *Adelaide and Theodore* (London: Pickering & Chatto, 2017)

HAYS, MARY, ED. BY GINA LURIA WALKER, *Appeal to the Men of Great Britain in behalf of Women* (New York: Garland, 1974)

HAYS, MARY, ED. BY GINA LURIA WALKER, *The Idea of Being Free: A Mary Hays Reader* (Toronto: Broadview Press, 2005)

ROLAND, MANON, ED. BY EVELYN SHUCKBURGH, *The Memoirs of Madame Roland, a Heroine of the French Revolution* (Kingston, Rhode Island: Moyer Bell, 1986)

ROUSSEAU, JEAN-JACQUES, *Émile or On Education*, trans. by Allan Bloom (New York: Basic Books, 1979)

WOLLSTONECRAFT, MARY, ED. BY JANET TODD, *A Vindication of the Rights of Woman* (Oxford: Oxford University Press, 2008)

Original Texts Online

JOHN BENNETT, <https://books.google.co.uk/books/about/Strictures_on_female_education.html?id=QSg8AAAAIAAJ>

HESTER CHAPONE, <https://books.google.co.uk/books/about/Letters_on_the_improvement_of_the_mind.html?id=h5QDAAAAQAAJ>

MARIA EDGEWORTH, <https://digital.library.upenn.edu/women/edgeworth/ladies/ladies.html>

JAMES FORDYCE, <https://books.google.co.uk/books/about/Sermons_to_young_women.html?id=EPvotQIhvH8C>

THOMAS GISBORNE, <https://books.google.co.uk/books/about/An_Enquiry_Into_the_Duties_of_the_Female.html?id=oDMEAAAAYAAJ>

MARY HAYS, <http://www.maryhayslifewritingscorrespondence.com/mary-hays-correspondence/mary-hays-s-writings/pamphlets-and-books/appeal-to-men-of-great-britain-1798>

HANNAH MORE, <https://books.google.co.uk/books/about/Strictures_on_the_Modern_System_of_Femal.html?id=3gKR8vkn8xAC>

JEAN-JACQUES ROUSSEAU, https://oll.libertyfund.org/title/rousseau-Émile-or-education

PRISCILLA WAKEFIELD, <https://books.google.co.uk/books/about/Reflections_on_the_Present_Condition_of.html?id=McRYAAAAcAAJ>

Further Reading

COOPER, DUFF, *Talleyrand* (London: Vintage Classics, 2010) [1st edn 1932]
DAVIES, KATE, *Catharine Macaulay & Mercy Otis Warren: The Revolutionary Atlantic and the Politics of Gender* (Oxford: Oxford University Press, 2005)
DEMERS, PATRICIA, *The World of Hannah More* (Lexington: Kentucky University Press, 1996)
FRANKLIN, CAROLINE, *Mary Wollstonecraft: A Literary Life* (Basingstoke: Palgrave Macmillan, 2004)
HILL, BRIDGET, *The Republican Virago: The Life and Times of Catharine Macaulay, Historian* (Oxford: Clarendon Press, 1992)
LAWDAY, DAVID, *Napoleon's Master: A Life of Prince Talleyrand* (London: Jonathan Cape, 2006)
MOORE, LUCY, *Liberty: The Lives and Times of Six Women in Revolutionary France* (London: Harper Perennial, 2007)
NARDIN, JANE, 'Hannah More and the Rhetoric of Educational Reform', *Women's History Review*, 10, 2, 2001, pp. 211–28
REYNOLDS, SIÂN, *Marriage and Revolution: Monsieur & Madame Roland* (Oxford: Oxford University Press, 2012)
STOTT, ANNE, *Hannah More: The First Victorian* (Oxford: Oxford University Press, 2003)
TAYLOR, BARBARA, *Mary Wollstonecraft and the Feminist Imagination* (Cambridge: Cambridge University Press, 2003)
TOMALIN, CLAIRE, *The Life and Death of Mary Wollstonecraft* (London: Penguin, 2012)
TROUILLE, MARY SEIDMAN, *Sexual Politics in the Enlightenment: Women Writers Read Rousseau* (New York: State University of New York Press, 1997)
WALKER, GINA LURIA, *Mary Hays: The Growth of a Woman's Mind* (London: Ashgate, 2006)
WOKLER, ROBERT, *Rousseau: A Very Short Introduction* (Oxford: Oxford University Press, 2001)

Online Resources

MARY HAYS, <http://www.maryhayslifewritingscorrespondence.com>

Lightning Source UK Ltd.
Milton Keynes UK
UKHW020123251121
394541UK00003B/116